CABINS & COTTAGES

OF CALIFORNIA

Tom & Marthea Thompson

Printed in the United States of America
First printing, 1994
Second printing, 1995
Third Printing, 2000

Send all inquiries to Publisher:
Rustic Getaways
P.O. Box 972,
Meadow Vista, CA 95722

Cabins & Cottages of California
ISBN 0-9641409-1-8
Cover and graphic design: Tom R. Thompson

Special thanks to Doneva S. Kaserman (for graphic contributions).

CONTENTS

NORTHERN COAST

LAKE TAHOE & VICINITY

SOUTHERN CALIFORNIA

NORTHERN REGION

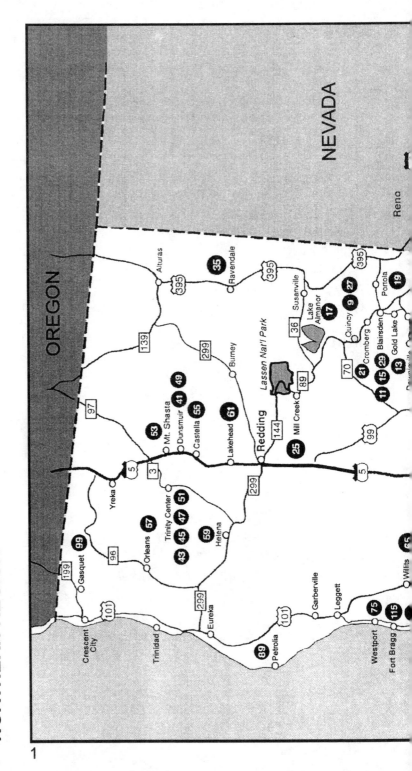

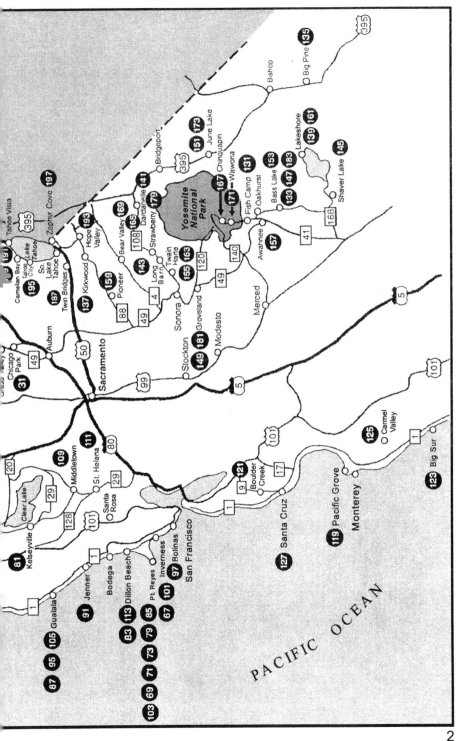

SOUTHERN REGION

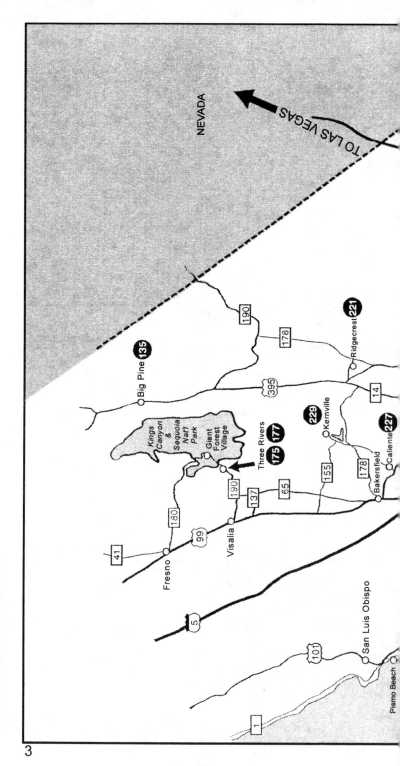

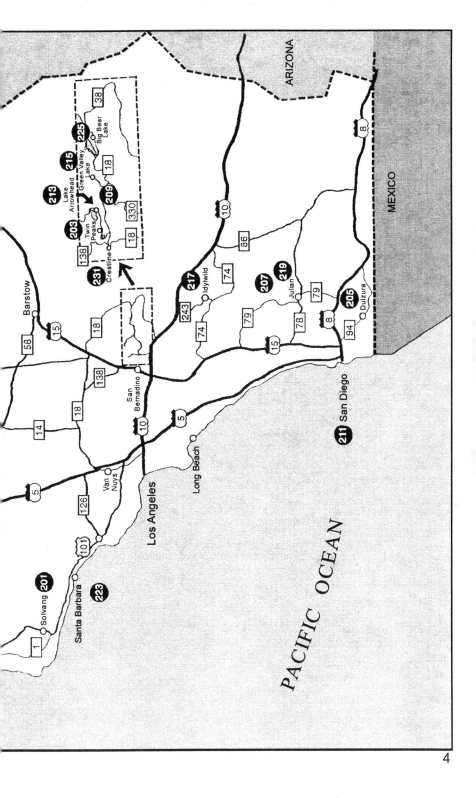

INTRODUCTION

Cabins & Cottages of California is a unique guide for those wishing to experience the ultimate in "Rustic Getaways." This book was inspired, primarily, from the variety of lodging experiences my wife and I have had in our travels throughout California - "experiences" I'm sure we have all had.

First, there's the "motel experience," which is basically sleeping in boxes, sometimes noisy, sometimes requiring the hauling of luggage up flights of stairs, and almost always without cooking facilities.   Then, there's the "camping experience," which includes sleeping (or not sleeping) on cold, hard ground, dealing with dust and dirt, usually with no facilities available to clean up, and nearby campers who have whining kids or enjoy loud music at 1 a.m.   Then, there's the traditional "bed and breakfast experience" which is very nice, but oftentimes expensive, and is usually limited to staying in a large house and sharing a bathroom and dining room with total strangers.

Finally, the experience that my wife and I have come to know and love is the "cabin and cottage experience." There are many advantages to these types of facilities. First, are the surroundings: most of the cabins and cottages we have enjoyed are located adjacent to peaceful rivers, moonlit lakes, redwood forests, or beautiful seascapes.

Second, is the advantage of quiet privacy, as most units are detached. Third, if you desire, is the ability to cook breakfast, lunch, or have a romantic candlelit dinner in your own private cabin or cottage. Finally, not only will you save money on meals, many of the lodging prices in this book are lower than a motel, and almost always less than a traditional bed and breakfast.

As you will notice, we have purposely decided to not "rate" each listing, as this can be very subjective. Thus, this handy guide is intended primarily as a reference source and, as such, we cannot guarantee total satisfaction to each lodging visitor.

However, we highly suggest that you contact the listing and request information prior to making reservations. We have found the owners and managers of these facilities to be warm and hospitable.

Happy lodging and we sincerely hope you enjoy your "Rustic Getaway!"

Tom & Marthea Thompson

NORTHERN SIERRA

Bucks Lake Marina

P.O. Box 559
Quincy, CA 95971
(530) 283-4243
Owners: DeWitt & Kim Henderson

Accommodations: 8 cabins, 18 RV sites, 6 camp sites.

Amenities: All have lake views, kitchens, baths (all basic kitchen supplies furnished), porches, and free boat launching for guests.

Rates: $60.00 - $75.00 per night.

Minimum Stay: Between June 1 and August 31 (one week), Sept 1 to June 30 (one night).

Restrictions: None

Bucks Lake Marina is nestled high up in the Plumas National Forest and overlooks beautiful Bucks Lake. It is located just a few hours from Sacramento, Reno, and Tahoe.

Bucks Lake, sometimes known as the "Jewel of the Sierra's", has 17 miles of shoreline, sandy beaches and tall pines offering something for everyone. During the summer, activities include water-skiing, sailing, fishing, hiking, swimming, and more. In the winter, snowmobiling, sledding and cross-country skiing.

We have eight housekeeping cabins named Dogwood, Aspen, Ash, Oak, Rainbow, Easternbrook, Lochleven, and Kokanee. All the cabins overlook the lake with a short path to the water's edge. The cabins are one or two bedroom and sleep from one to five persons. Pets are allowed at an additional cost.

The cabins are rustic and cozy and have kitchens and baths. The kitchens are supplied with all the basic utensils, coffee percolators, and full size refrigerators. We supply the bedding and the first set of towels.

Bucks Lake Marina also has RV sites with full hook ups, all with lake views. They are rented seasonally, but after Labor Day we have openings. Many people enjoy the fall with the great fishing and our colorful Dogwood and Aspen trees. We have campsites as well, available all summer.

Our resort has full dock facilities including a launch ramp, dock slips, gasoline and oil for boats. We offer free boat launching for our guests. We rent fishing boats, pontoon boats, kayaks, canoes, and personal watercrafts. Whether lake or stream fishing you can catch Rainbows, German Browns, Mackinaw, Kokanee, and Brook Trout.

There is a restaurant that is within walking distance, a general store, bar and game room. Horseback riding is located within one half mile of our resort.

Bucks Lake offers a unique vacation experience. Most people who visit reserve again for the following year. We look forward to seeing you at Bucks Lake.

The Feather River Inn

P.O. Box 67
Graeagle, CA 96103-0062
(530) 836-2623
Owner: University of the Pacific

Accommodations: 55 rooms, cabins, and chalets.

Amenities: Golf course, pool, and tennis court.

Rates: $44.00 - $120.00

Minimum Stay: One night.

Restrictions: No pets.

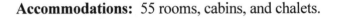

Built in 1914 by the First Interstate Company of Chicago, this charming alpine style lodge has some 13 cabins and chalets. There is also a dormitory that accommodates 38 persons. The Feather River Inn is an American Plan facility for groups as well as individuals (individuals may purchase meals when groups are here).

Once the rival of the Awanhee Hotel (in Yosemite), this Inn was donated to the University of the Pacific in the early 1960's. The University turned operation of the Inn over to the Alumni Association after it ceased operating the site as a prep school.

This area has been described by many travel writers as the best kept secret of the Sierras. Easily reached via the Reno/Lake Tahoe airport in Reno and 2.5 hours driving time from Sacramento to the Graeagle area, this Inn offers beautiful scenery, a relaxing atmosphere, 3 championship golf courses, 3 attractive 9 hole courses, dozens of high mountain lakes, tennis, horseback riding trails and rental horses, guided fishing trips, and great snowmobiling in the winter. The Inn offers a variety of special seminars in photography, computers, quilting and needlework, history, and cultural interest studies.

Gold Lake Lodge

P.O. Box 25
Graeagle, CA 96103
(530) 836-2350
www.goldlakelodge.com
Owners: Ann & Pete Thill

Accommodations: Individual cabins with queen, double and twin beds.

Amenities: Cozy mountain lodge, beautiful ancient trees, alpine meadows, sunsets, and friendly folks.

Rates: $95.00 - $180.00 per night.   Dinner and breakfast included; lunch by request.

Minimum Stay: Two nights. Weekly rates are available.

Restrictions: No pets.   Smoking allowed outdoors only.   No TV.

Gold Lake Lodge is an unpretentious old-fashioned mountain lodge. Gold Lake Lodge has been in continuous operation since the spring of 1912. We have been selected for nomination into the National Register of Historic Places.

The Lodge is relatively small. When all eleven cabins are full, we have approximately 28 guests. Cabin rentals include a hearty breakfast and four course dinners, daily maid service to keep everything neat and tidy, full linens, and whatever hospitality the Lodge staff can provide you. Fine wines and bottled beers are always available for purchase as well as sodas and mineral water. The Lodge is blessed with pure, sweet, mountain spring water.

Activities include outdoor ping-pong, tetherball, horseshoes, volleyball, and badminton. The finest trails into the Lakes Basin backcountry begin at your cabin porch. Thirty natural mountain lakes are within reach of the hiker. The closest to the Lodge is Big Bear Lake, a mere 1/4 mile walk. Fishing, photography, and exploring old mining ruins are favorite pastimes of guests, many of whom have been visiting for three generations.

If you decide it is time for a "break," our main lodge provides a quiet, cozy place to read or visit with the rest of us.

If you prefer a change of pace, Graeagle is just 15 minutes away at the base of the mountain. Here you will find four beautiful golf courses, shopping, tennis, and stables.

So...come enjoy our beautiful mountaintop with alpine meadows at your step. Gold Lake Lodge offers the best in outdoor enjoyment. The Lodge operates under special use permit with the Plumas National Forest.

Gray Eagle Lodge

P.O. Box 38
Blairsden, CA 96103
(530) 836-2511
(800) 635-8778
Owner: Richard Smith

Accommodations: 15 cabins (one & two bedrooms) with full bathrooms and decks.

Amenities: Cozy log lodge with living, dining, game rooms, and full bar.

Rates: $120.00 - $255.00 per night. (Daily rates include cabin, breakfast, dinner, and daily maid service.)

Minimum Stay: Three nights.

Restrictions: Open from May to October. No TV or phone (telephone in main lodge).

A hearty, warm welcome from the Smith family is what you can expect when you arrive at the Gray Eagle Lodge. Make yourself at home. Take in the incredible scenery surrounding the lodge, breathe in the sweet mountain air, and listen to the quiet. Your vacation has begun.

You may choose to kick back, nap, or read a book; however, if you want to jump right into action, you might have a tough time deciding where to begin. Hiking adventures begin right at your doorstep. Dozens of mountain peaks surround the lodge for hiking or just strolling. There are trails for all levels of physical activity.

Tell a tale. We always keep champagne on ice just in case we hear a good fish story. There's no problem finding a place to fish around here. On up the trail are 40 alpine lakes where those fish are just waiting to outsmart you.

Ace a hole. Just minutes from the lodge are the beautiful and challenging Plumas Pines and Graeagle Meadows, two 18-hole championship courses. There are two nine-hole courses nearby also.

Kick trail. Mountain bikers rave about the trail system that surrounds the lodge, and the views are outrageous.

Kid around. There are plenty of wholesome outdoor activities including the best swimming hole, rubber rafting, and sand play. There are also games, puzzles, ping-pong, pool, billiards, and other table games for your entertainment.

Horse around at any of the three outstanding stables in the area.

Snap it. For photographers, the scope of subjects seems endless: panoramic vistas, wildflowers, beautiful fall colors, birds, and critters.

All of this is nestled in the Plumas National Forest, four and a half hours from the Bay Area and one hour from Reno.

Lake Almanor Vacation Rentals

CENTURY 21/
Lake Almanor Real Estate
499 Peninsula Drive
Lake Almanor, CA 96137
(530) 596-4386
(530) 596-3475 (FAX)

Accommodations: Forty cabins and homes.

Amenities: Completely furnished and well-equipped with outside decks, deck furniture, and BBQ'S. Swimming, tennis, golf, boat launching, and picnic areas.

Rates: $400.00 to $1,575.00 per week.

Minimum Stay: One week during summer months (Saturday - Saturday).

Restrictions: No pets are allowed. Most require smoking outside only.

Lake Almanor is a beautiful 52-square mile lake located in Plumas County at an elevation of 4,500 feet. Lake Almanor is approximately 2 1/2 hours northwest of Reno, about 3 1/2 hours north of Sacramento and about 5 1/2 hours northeast of San Francisco. Lake Almanor can be reached via Highways 395 & 36, or 70 & 89, or I-5 & Highway 36 or I-5 & Highway 32.

In addition to Lake Almanor, there are several other smaller lakes and streams in the area. In total, this area offers some of the finest fishing in Northern California. Lake Almanor is also ideal for other water sports such as swimming, sailing, water skiing or just plain sightseeing. Mt. Lassen National Park is a short 40-minute drive away.

Total rental fees are to be paid prior to arrival and are refundable if cancelled more than 30 days before commencement date. Upon arrival it will be necessary to check in with CENTURY 21/Lake Almanor Real Estate. You may request specific rental units complete with photographs by calling our office.

Renters must provide their own linens. Everything else including blankets is provided. Information on the number of beds and bed sizes will be furnished upon request. All homes have outside sun decks, BBQ's, and deck furniture. Each home has a limit as to the number of guests the home will accommodate.

Lake Almanor Country Club boat launching facilities are located in the Recreation Areas and are for day use only. There is a charge of $20.00 per week for any boat brought into the country club. Tennis and golf are available as well.

Shopping is available within a two to ten mile radius and includes grocery stores, sporting goods, gasoline, hardware, marine supplies, clothing, and a drug store. The surrounding areas have over ten churches and a fully staffed hospital.

Lake Davis Resort

P.O. Box 1385
Portola, CA 96122
(530) 832-1060
www.lakedavisresort.com
Owners: Tony & Sylvia Olson

Accommodations: 3 one bedroom cabins (2 - 4 people) and 1 two bedroom cabin (4 - 8 people).

Amenities: Housekeeping cabins with full kitchens, microwaves, dishwashers, kerosene heaters, and open view pellet stoves for a romantic atmosphere.

Rates: Summer: 1 bedroom ($78.00), 2 bedroom ($120.00); Winter: 1 bedroom ($85.00), 2 bedroom ($127.00).
Children: ages 3-15, $5.00 a night; over age 16, $10.00 a night.
All rates subject to a 9% room tax, 50% deposit required.

Minimum Stay: Two nights

Restrictions: No pets. No smoking.

Lake Davis Resort includes brand new housekeeping cabins located in a game reserve, and only 1/4 mile from Lake Davis. They are secluded in the pines, at an elevation of 6,000 feet, but only 55 miles northwest of Reno, Nevada.

All cabins have open beam ceilings, queen beds and hide-a-beds, full bathrooms and kitchens, including dishwashers and microwaves. A handicapped unit is also available.

Snuggle in front of the open view pellet stove with the one you love or go cross-country skiing, biking, hiking, fishing, horseback riding, swimming, tennis, or boating. You can also enjoy sports such as sleigh rides, snowmobiling, snowman building, or driving a diesel train engine nearby.

This is a great romantic getaway for two or for family fun. Just bring your food and toothbrush. Restaurants and stores are within a 15-minute drive.

Other things to see in the area include the Railroad Museum, Railroad Days, 4th of July celebration, Arts & Crafts Fair, County Fair, Plumas-Eureka State Park, Bucks Lake Wilderness area, historic mining towns such as Seneca and Rich Bar, Lassen National Park, and the Pacific Crest Trail.

Long Valley Resort

59532 Highway 70
Cromberg, CA 96103
(530) 836-0754
www.longvalleyresort.com
Owners: Bryan and Stephanie Sprague

Accommodations: Modern, fully furnished 1, 2, and 3 bedroom cottages with queen-sized beds.

Amenities: Each kitchen is fully equipped including a microwave. All of the cottages are air-conditioned. Towels and bed linen are provided with semi-weekly maid service. Cottage #2 is barrier free with a roll shower.

Rates: $59.50 (one bedroom), $64.50 (two bedroom), $79.50 nightly (three bedroom); $380.00, $410.00, $500.00 weekly.

Minimum Stay: Two nights.

Restrictions: No pets. Smoking outdoors only.

Long Valley Resort and the Feather River wonderland await you! Conveniently located on Highway 70, "The Feather River Scenic Byway", we are a terrific place to rest and relax. The resort is tucked away in a forest of pine, cedar, and fir. This quiet setting is perfect for family reunions, picnics, and relaxation under the trees or just a great place to watch one of our mountain sunsets.

Nearby Graeagle is a golfer's paradise. Six picturesque courses are ready to challenge every golfer. Tennis and excellent horseback riding facilities are also found in and around Graeagle.

Plumas County is filled with year round outdoor adventures. The Long Valley Resort in Cromberg is right in the center of great fishing from the wild and scenic Middle Fork of the Feather River, great hiking, or the wonderful colors of fall. After the snow falls, the newly renovated Ski Gold Mountain promises to be great family fun for skiers of all abilities.

While the day's catch is grilling on your deck's barbecue, you might want to challenge your family to a game of horsehoes or volleyball under the shade of our pine forest.

Far removed from the hustle and bustle of the city, the Long Valley Resort in Cromberg is the perfect place to spend a weekend of uninterrupted time creating a heritage scrapbook or working on a family heirloom quilt.

The Long Valley Resort is open year round. We are just 10 minutes west of the Graeagle turnoff, on Highway 70, a short one-hour drive from Reno. Cromberg is 15 miles east of Quincy. We are an easy drive from Sacramento or the Bay Area. Hope to see you soon!

The Lure Resort

Highway 49
P.O. Box 95
Downieville, CA 95936
(530) 289-3465, (800) 671-4084
www.lureresort.com
Owners: Gary and Linda Zolldan

Accommodations: Housekeeping cabins: Nine completely furnished and well-equipped one and two bedroom cabins with kitchen and bathroom on the North Yuba River. Most cabins have spacious decks with barbecue and patio furniture overlooking the river. Log Camping cabins: Eight cabins on the river's edge. Each has a log double bed and log bunk bed accommodating a maximum of four guests. Every site has an open fire pit/barbecue and picnic table. Bring your own linens. Central restroom with flush toilets and hot shower.

Amenities: Fourteen riverfront acres, fishing, gold panning, swimming and hiking.

Rates: $50.00 - $195.00 depending on cabin and number of guests. Pets $15.00 each per night.

Minimum Stay: Seasonal variation.

Restrictions: Smoking outside only. Pets must be on leash while on resort grounds.

Nestled in the Tahoe National Forest one mile east of Downieville along scenic Highway 49, the Lure Resort is a peaceful retreat in a tranquil Sierra setting. Leave your cares and woes behind you as you cross the Lure Resort Bridge and enter fourteen beautiful riverfront acres offering lovely log cabins on the banks of the North Yuba River. This is a nature lover's paradise where wildlife and beauty abound.

Our housekeeping cabins come fully equipped with kitchen facilities and linens. Our new deluxe cabins offer vaulted ceilings, expansive glass, pine interiors and living/dining rooms with a cozy gas log parlor stove. Kitchens are fully equipped as well. Bathrooms are full sized with tub/shower combo. There are large decks with barbecue and patio furniture.

Come to the Lure to relax and enjoy a day in the sun while fishing, swimming, gold panning or hiking. Visit the historical towns of Downieville and Sierra City where groceries, gifts, antiques, restaurants and services are available.

The Lure Resort is just minutes west of Bassett's Station and the Lakes Basin where numerous crystal clear alpine lakes lay peacefully below the shadows of the majestic Sierra Buttes. The Lure Resort is a historical property from the days of "49" where fortune hunters struck it rich mining in tunnels or panning along the banks of the Yuba River in search of the elusive precious metal, GOLD! You, too, may feel the fever and pan for gold yourself along the banks of the Yuba river. Come spend your vacation with us. The fishing is great and the hospitality first rate. You can try your luck at gold panning, or just relax and do some sun tanning. Go for a hike or ride a bike. It's so much fun at the Lure, you must stay for sure.

Mill Creek Resort

#1 Hwy. 172
Mill Creek, CA 96061
(530) 595-4449, (888) 595-4449
Owners: Terry & Georgene Neher

Accommodations: 9 cabins (one and two bedrooms).

Amenities: Cabins come with bathroom and kitchen facilities (cooking and eating utensils provided), linens, and gas heat. One cabin has a fireplace. Pets are welcome.

Rates: $50.00 - $70.00 per night.

Minimum Stay: One night.

Restrictions: Operated on National Forest use permit.

Mill Creek Resort is located in the Southern Cascades, 11 miles from the southwest entrance to Lassen Volcanic National Park. At an elevation of 4,800 feet there is a variety of large trees, fresh air, and cold mountain streams. Wildlife ranges from deer to raccoons, squirrels, and more.

The resort is near Mill Creek, which originates in Lassen Park and flows to the Sacramento River, near Red Bluff. Smaller creeks run beside the cabins. Mill Creek is a catch-and-release trout stream.

The summer provides fishing in local creeks and hiking in Lassen Park. Winter provides a quiet beauty for Nordic skiing and a variety of winter snow play.

These individual one and two bedroom rustic cabins sleep from one to six people.

The main building of the resort has a small grocery store with basic dry goods. In the same building there is a small coffee shop serving breakfast, lunch, and dinner. There is a beautiful outdoor deck open in the summer for meals.

So come and see for yourself.

> At our Mill Creek Resort,
>   in the winter there's snow.
> In summer it's green,
>   and cool waters flow.
> Enjoy with us
>   Mother Nature sublime,
> and come up and
>   see us sometime!

The little resort at Mill Creek is almost as old as the hills. Same good friends every year. It's out of the way where it's <u>not</u> happening.

Paxton Lodge

P.O. Box 3367
Quincy, CA 95971
(530) 283-1141
(530) 283-0313 FAX
Owners: Ronald & Jane Schwartz/Ronald Pound

Accommodations: Rooms in lodge.

Amenities: Pool table, ping pong table, horseshoe pits, and laundry facilities.

Rates: $35.00 - $45.00 per night.

Minimum Stay: One day.

Restrictions: No smoking. No pets.

Paxton Lodge is a unique hideaway located in the spectacular Feather River Canyon. If you would like to get away from the rush of the city life and kick back to enjoy the slower pace of the past, this is still achievable at Paxton Lodge. Twentieth century pressures evaporate amid the tranquil charm of a former era. The surrounding country still remains just as in the pioneer days when the miners and prospectors roamed these mountains in search for gold.

An expansive view of the Feather River Canyon and surrounding mountains creates a special magic for guests as they relax at this former railroad resort. This resort was built in 1917 by the Indian Valley Railroad and operated as an executive resort in the canyon until 1938. It is currently being restored to its original splendor. The Union Pacific today operates through the historic Feather River Canyon. Enjoy modern railroading in the Canyon and the "Keddie Wye".

The surrounding area offers golf courses, hiking among the fragrant pine trees, trout fishing in the Feather River, or in an unlimited number of streams and lakes in the area. Winter sports include downhill skiing at Johnsville, cross-country skiing, and snowmobiling.

We have four river view, and four forest view rooms offering a romantic setting. The rooms are accented with a potpourri of furnishings from throughout the lodge era. Each room has been equipped with a queen or a full size bed, comforter, and is available with private or shared bath.

River Pines Resort

P.O. Box 117
Blairsden, CA 96103
(530) 836-2552
(530) 836-0815 FAX
Owners: Jim & Leslie Ross

Accommodations: 30 deluxe motel units, 14 original motel units, and 18 housekeeping cottages.

Amenities: Swimming pool, hot tub, ping pong, shuffleboard, horseshoes, and dining room.

Rates: $50.00 - $215.00 per night.

Minimum Stay: One night (motels). Three nights (cottages).

Restrictions: No pets.

River Pines Resort is located in the beautiful Mohawk Valley in Plumas County. We are 50 miles north of Truckee, 60 miles west of Reno and accessible all year long. Highway 70, the lowest point across the Sierras, is only one mile away.

We are just outside the town of Graeagle. The area has two 18 hole golf courses and two 9 hole golf courses, located within two miles of the resort.

Fishing in the Lakes Basin area is popular during the summer months. The Middle Fork of the Feather River borders our 17 acres and is a great place for fly-fishing. Our accommodations vary. In our "original" motel units we offer rooms with mini kitchens as well as suites. In our "deluxe" units, we offer spacious one and two bedroom suites (kitchens are available). Our housekeeping cottages are one and two bedrooms and come fully equipped with kitchen amenities and linens.

Come and relax at River Pines Resort. We will make your stay an enjoyable one.

Rollins Lakeside Inn

P.O. Box 152
Chicago Park, CA 95712
(530) 273-0729
Owners: Larry & Pat Hudson

Accommodations: 9 individual cabins.

Amenities: Pool with lake access, volleyball, and game room with pool table.

Rates: $70.00 - $125.00 per night, (weekly rates available).

Minimum Stay: Two nights.

Restrictions: None.

Rollins Lakeside Inn is nestled in the foothills just two and a half hours from San Francisco and one hour from Sacramento. We offer completely furnished cabins with color TV's (including the Movie Channel), complete kitchens, all linens, and Weber barbecues on each porch.

There is access to the lake for fishing, boating, and swimming. The Club Room is equipped with a pool table. Enjoy horseshoes, volleyball, or group barbecues in our recreation area.

We are just minutes from historic Grass Valley, Nevada City, Yuba, Bear, and American Rivers.

We are a small family resort. Cabins can accommodate up to 8 people. Weekly rates are reduced from $400.00 to $600.00 per week.

For a secluded getaway experience, please visit us at the Rollins Lakeside Inn.

Sierra Shangri-La

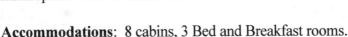

P.O. Box 285
Downieville, CA 95936
(530) 289-3455
Innkeepers: Fran & Frank Car

Accommodations: 8 cabins, 3 Bed and Breakfast rooms.

Amenities: Woodstoves in cabins, large meeting room with fireplace.

Rates: $54.00 - $121.00 per night.

Minimum Stay: Cabins available on a weekly basis in June, July, and August. No minimum for Bed and Breakfast rooms.

Restrictions: Cabins (smoking on deck only). Bed and Breakfast rooms are smoke-free. No pets.

Shangri-La is a small resort on the North Fork of the Yuba River in the Sierra Nevada Range of California at 3,100 feet elevation, carved out of the mountainside at the exact spot where Crow City once was a rip-roaring mining camp.

Shangri-La is at the base of Jim Crow Canyon, where the crystal clear water from the ravine pushes gently into the Yuba. From Jim Crow Canyon, for 1,800 feet, is the magnificent Shangri-La wall made of native river stone. On the edge of the wall, with views up and down the river, are three cottages: BlueJay, La

Vista, and Flycaster. Jim Crow overlooks both Jim Crow Creek and the Yuba River. Nestled in the tall pine, fir, and cedar trees are Dogwood Manor, Cedar Ridge, and El Dorado. La Siesta is a cozy unit adjacent to the main lodge. On the upper level of the lodge are three bed and breakfast units with balconies having unobstructed views of the river.

The evening breeze from the canyon makes it impossible for you not to unwind and completely relax. As the water of the Yuba cascades past your doorstep, affording the ultimate in Rainbow and German Brown angling, it also furnishes the lullaby to assist you to sleep.

We do assure you that you will particularly like the peace and tranquility here beside the Yuba River.

Spanish Springs Ranch

P.O. Box 70
Ravendale, CA 96123
(530) 234-2150
(530) 234-2041 FAX
Owners: Jim & Sharon Vondracek

Accommodations: 4 log cabins and 13 suites with kitchens.

Amenities: Linens, cooking and eating utensils, bathrooms, and horses.

Rates: $60.00 - $145.00 per night.

Minimum Stay: One night.

Restrictions: None.

The Spanish Springs Territory is a collection of landholdings and ranches scattered across California's Madeline Plains and the high desert country over to the top of Nevada's remote Black Rock Desert.

Our main headquarters will provide a more 20th century western vacation, while our remote ranches and homesteads (the Mar, the Evans, the Horne, Cold Springs, and Soldier Meadows) will take you back in time and provide an authentic working ranch environment.

In addition to riding and fishing, guests may enjoy our private swimming pool, tennis, volleyball, shuffleboard, and children's playground. There is a petting zoo of small animals, horseshoe pits, archery, hayrides, cookouts, campfires, and western barbecues.

Other activities include cattle drives, horse drives, and roundups; or you can ride the trails with our wranglers, in the tradition of the "old west".

Sleeping accommodations range from roomy lodge pole cabins, duplex units, and finely appointed suites with living rooms and private baths to the bunkhouse offering boys and girls dormitories, game room, and private rooms for mom and dad.

At Spanish Springs Ranch you can be close to the action, but far enough away to appreciate the serenity and beauty of this rugged high desert country.

Yuba River Inn

P.O. Box 236
Sierra City, CA 96125
(530) 862-1122
www.yubariverinn.com
Owners: The Hertzberg Family

Accommodations: Log and non-log cabins, 7 with fully equipped kitchens. Open all year.

Amenities: All cabins furnished with towels, bedding, sheets and linens. New two bedroom cabins coming soon.

Rates: $45.00 - $130.00 per night. Pets $10.00 per night.

Minimum Stay: Three nights in summer. Two nights off season.

Restrictions: Pets must have bedding, leash, and carrier if possible. No credit cards accepted.

The Yuba River Inn is a resort nestled at the base of the majestic Sierra Buttes rising to an altitude of 8,589 feet. The North Fork of the Yuba River flows at the back door of the Inn.

All ten cabins are named after native trees that grow on the resort. These cabins are named: Oak, Cedar, Fir, Spruce, Pine,

Alder, Madrone, Wildplum, Aspen, and Ponderosa.

Mark Twain, once a contributing writer for our local newspaper, the Mountain Messenger, described the area as finding the air "as pure and fine bracing and beautifully clear," and why shouldn't it be for it's the same air as the angels breathe heavenly pine-scented mountain air.

Soak up the sun at the resort pool with a view of the Sierra Buttes or grab a fly rod and fish a 1/3 mile of private river frontage just below the cabins. There are numerous trails to hike in the mountain lake area and miles of streams providing the finest trout fishing.

Our non-kitchen cabins have small refrigerators for cold drinks and private baths with stall showers. Our single bedroom cabins with full kitchens have either double and twin beds or queen and twin beds. Two of the cabins have built-in BBQ'S.

Our large two bedroom cabins come with living rooms and kitchens. They all have one bedroom with one queen and one twin bed, and the second bedroom has one double and one twin bed. All have full porch patios and BBQ'S. One cabin (Wild Plum) comes with a wood-burning stove and whirlpool bath.

Activities include fishing, hiking, bird-watching, snowmobiling, canoeing, gold panning, cross-country skiing, and Kentucky-Mine concerts. Restaurants and stores are within a ten-minute walk. A place to remember long after packing up and returning home is the Yuba River Inn.

SHASTA/TRINITY

Best in the West Resort

26925 Sims Rd. I-5 & Sims Exit (W)
Castella, CA 96017
(530) 235-2603
e-mail: eggerbestwest.webtv.net
www.eggerbestwest.com
Owners: The Egger Family

Accommodations: 5 cottages and 12 trailer spaces.

Amenities: Woodstoves, kitchens, and access to all weather sports.

Rates: $45.00 (and up) per night. Stay for 3 days or more and receive a discount.

Minimum Stay: One night.

Restrictions: Pets ok. Smoking outside only.

The Best in the West Resort is a small resort nestled in the Sacramento Canyon among the pines, cedars, and firs with majestic Mount Shasta 20 miles to the north, the Sacramento River and Interstate 5 one quarter of a mile to the east, and magnificent Lake Shasta about twenty miles to the south.

This special, peaceful spot is situated alongside of crystal clear Mears Creek gurgling to the Sacramento River, in the midst of animals and birds in the forests. Walks may be taken to observe the wildlife and smell the wildflowers. Azaleas scent the air in the spring. Blackberries are abundant in summer.

The Sacramento River affords many activities: white water rafting, innertubing, swimming and family play, and limited fishing.

Many day trips may be made to surrounding areas. Within a few minutes drive, one may Alpine or cross-country ski, golf, hike, climb crags, water-ski, swim, go for a peaceful walk, or sit and read a book in the shade.

Five modern cottages (one or two bedrooms) are arranged around a courtyard bordering the peaceful creek. All have complete kitchens with gas ranges and wood-heating stoves, with full baths, back decks which have been recently redecorated, with an occupancy of 2-6 persons. All the modern necessities are available without the bustle of city life. In short, this is a retreat.

A small R.V. park is on the property with beautifully landscaped shaded sites. Laundry facilities, L.P. Gas and public phone are on the property.

We are building a family lodge which should be done in summer 2000 for reunions. It will hold approximately 12-15 people. Come up and visit and make this your special retreat.

Bonanza King Resort

Rt 2, Box 4790
Trinity Center, CA 96091
(530) 266-3305
www.bonanzakingresort.com
Owners: Mike & Nanette Ransom

Accommodations: 7 widely spaced housekeeping cabins, sleeping from three to seven people, all with patios or decks, picnic tables and barbecues. Open all year.

Amenities: Complete kitchens, linens and towels provided. Over 1,200 feet of Coffee Creek running through property, excellent fishing, and an old-time swimming hole. Hike into scenic Trinity Alps. Children's play area.

Rates: $70 - $80 per night (one or two person rate). Each extra person $10.00.

Minimum Stay: Weekly blocks of time June 10 to Labor Day. Two-night minimum off-season. Major holidays three night minimum.

Restrictions: Smoking outside only. No pets allowed.

Our small resort is on eight beautiful acres along Coffee Creek -- a large, lovely stream fed by snow from the Trinity Alps.

Filled with natural beauty and abundant wildlife, it has been designated a Wilderness Area by the U.S. Government.

We take pride in offering a clean and quiet setting for your vacation. We offer seven fully furnished and equipped cabins, some with woodstoves, some with sleeping lofts, all clean and private. Guests will enjoy our grounds with plenty of green grass, flower beds in natural settings, sitting areas with chaises and hammocks, a play area with a swingset, sandbox, playhouse, badminton, basketball hoop, ping pong, horseshoe pit, and volleyball. We have a large campfire for impromptu gatherings, and stargazing. Vegetable gardens and wandering chickens and ducks complete the picture.

With over 1,200 feet of frontage along our property, Coffee Creek offers something for everyone. Fishermen will find excellent sport with Rainbow Trout and the occasional large German Brown. The dreamer and reader will enjoy the quiet beauty, and everyone enjoys our wonderful swimming hole.

For the more adventuresome, there are many beautiful hikes strewn with wildflowers, as well as spectacular mountain lakes.

Some folks like to boat and fish large Trinity Lake (Clair Engle Lake) just three miles away. Boat rentals are available. The Bonanza King Resort is a six hour drive from the Bay Area, therefore, our trails and lakes remain uncrowded.

Coffee Creek Chalet

Star Route 2-3968
Trinity Center, CA 96091
(530) 266-3235, fax (530) 266-3933
e-mail: rckausen@life-education.com
www.coffeecreekchalet.com
Owners: Robert & Dee Dee Kausen

Accommodations: Fully equipped vacation home.

Amenities: Fireplace, fishing, hiking, and cross-country skiing.

Rates: $135.00/night; $875.00/week for up to 4 people.

Minimum Stay: Two nights. Three nights on holidays.

Restrictions: Smoking outdoors only. No pets allowed.

An enchanting, peaceful quality surrounds this unique vacation home where the Trinity Alps meet Coffee Creek. The Coffee Creek Chalet offers you the peacefulness of nature with complete modern living convenience. If you want to get away, to unwind and take time to become more in tune with nature, then we know you will fall in love with this beautiful setting.

The Coffee Creek Chalet is less than a two-hour drive northwest of Redding, or southwest of Medford and just north of Trinity Lake. It is nestled among firs and cedars on three acres along Coffee Creek with thousands of acres of timberland as a backyard.

The Coffee Creek Chalet is a fully furnished, clean vacation home that can sleep four. Many of our personal treasures and belongings make it more a private residence than a rental. Downstairs is a bedroom with queen bed, a fully equipped kitchen, washer and dryer, and a bathroom with tub/shower. The cathedral ceiling living room offers a toasty wood-burning stove. (Yes, there's a gas heater in case you don't want to play fire builder.) Upstairs is an open loft with two twin beds. There is a VCR for movies, and a stereo/radio with cassette/CD deck. We supply all linens and towels.

Most folks come here to relax, read, and do nothing. Fishermen find this area a delight. You can catch native Rainbow Trout in Coffee Creek, or planters in the nearby Trinity River. Trinity Lake still holds the record for small mouth bass. There you'll also find large Rainbow, German Browns, Kokanee, large mouth bass, and catfish. The marina in Trinity Center (8 miles south) provides a free boat launch ramp and rents fishing boats.

There are numerous alpine lakes throughout the area where you can catch Brookies or just spend a leisurely afternoon enjoying nature at its best. Hikers will find dozens of day hikes offering varying degrees of difficulty. There is a tennis court at the nearby school, croquet, and horseshoes at the Chalet. In the winter, you can cross-country ski in many nearby areas.

Coffee Creek Ranch

4940 Coffee Creek Rd., Dept. RG
Trinity Center, CA 96091-9502
(530) 266-3343
(530) 266-3597 FAX
(800) 624-4480
Owners: Mark & Ruth Hartman

Accommodations: 14 cabins (one and two bedroom), porches, private baths with tub and showers, and wood-burning stoves with a view of the fire. Handicap ranch house room and facilities are available.

Amenities: Heated swimming pool, health spa, archery and rifle range, trapshoot, ping-pong, horseshoes, guided nature hikes, youth program from 3-17 during the summer season, badminton, volleyball, shuffleboard, basketball, pedal boating, fly-fishing, and horseback riding.

Rates: $250.00 - $924.00 per person per week (off-season rates available, specials, and senior discounts).

Minimum Stay: One week summer season. Two day minimum stay all other times.

Restrictions: None.

Relax on our 127 acre ranch surrounded by the Trinity Alps

Wilderness Area. Our retreat lies along Coffee Creek, an excellent trout stream for natives! We are located 72 miles northwest of Redding, three miles above Trinity Lake and five miles up Coffee Creek Road.

Our terrain begins at 3,100 feet, at the bottom of the river canyon, where spring brings kayaking and wildflowers, to our highest point, Billy's Peak at 7,200 feet, a three-hour hike.

Fish in Trinity Lake for large and smallmouth bass, Catfish, German Browns, Rainbow Trout, and King Salmon or take an all-day ride to a wilderness lake for some tasty brook trout!

Invigorating breakfast rides begin in the spring and end with fall colors. Yet another vacation experience we offer is wilderness pack trips for hunting (June through October), to just plain get away from it all!

Winter promotes a romantic "fairyland" setting while improving your Nordic skiing. Don't ski? Well, join the kids on Shotgun Hill for a race to the bottom on inner tubes or challenge them to a snowman building contest.

No matter what time of the year, there are always three meals a day either in the dining room or down by the pool for a BBQ, out on the trail for lunch or breakfast, or overnight at the lake. Gold panning and our band, the "Rattlesnakes," will entertain you year-round, but our hospitality and staff will keep you coming back for the hayride, bonfire, and more! There is "A Reason for Every Season" at Coffee Creek for you to be here. Many happy memories await you.

Dunsmuir Cabins

4727 Dunsmuir Ave.
Dunsmuir, CA 96025
(530) 235-2721
(888) 235-2721
Owners: Louie Dewey & Belinda Hanson

Accommodations: Cabins & houses.

Amenities: Pool, hot tub, fireplace, laundry, river front, and kitchens.

Rates: $33.00 - $150.00 per night.

Minimum Stay: One night.

Restrictions: Varies from property to property.

"A River Runs Through It" is not only the name of a great motion picture, it is also the definitive description of Dunsmuir, and Dunsmuir Cabins. Nestled in a forested canyon in the shadow of majestic Mt. Shasta, all of the Dunsmuir Cabins are either on the river or only a short walk away. That means fishing, hiking, biking, swimming, gold panning, and lazing in the sun in the summer; and skiing, snow boarding (some radical down- hill/cross-country runs are free), ice fishing, ice skating, and lazing in front of the fire in the winter. Every cabin has a completely furnished kitchen, but for the cook's night off, we are extremely fortunate to have an array of fabulous restaurants with menu items from Thailand to Germany and wine lists with everything from "Steelhead Beer" to "Dom Perione."

All of the Dunsmuir Cabins are unique and cover a wide range of styles. There are inexpensive rustic one or two-bedroom California Box Construction cabins that start at $33.00 a night. There are brand new units and antique furnished units that cost $150.00 a night. All of the names are revealing. Edit St. Guest House has the Shasta View Country unit and the Eddy Bauer cabin. Alaska Ranch has two cabins down river named after their favorite horse stock, Angel's Heaven and Fred's Palace (Fred is the mule). River House is just too obvious but you really can catch a fish in the back yard, and land it on the BBQ grill.

One of the best features of Dunsmuir is that you can reach this uncrowded paradise in a matter of hours even on the busiest of traffic days because I-5 is never bumper to bumper. We've got the getaway you want and a toll-free number. Give us a call!

Enright Gulch Cabins & Motel

3500 Hwy. 3
P.O. Box 244
Trinity Center, CA 96091
(530) 266-3600, (888) 383-5583
e-mail: gheilig@snowcrest.net
Owners: Gary Heilig

Accommodations: 4 housekeeping cabins and 2 motel units.

Amenities: Cabins have fully equipped kitchens and linens. Some have woodstoves and all have a porch or deck. Motel units have refrigerators, hot pots for coffee, and air conditioning.

Rates: Cabins ($70.00 - $80.00 per night); $5.00 each additional person. Motels ($40.00 - $45.00 per night).

Minimum Stay: Cabins (three days for advanced reservations May 15 - September 15). We accept drop-in overnighters in cabins when available. Motels (no minimum).

Restrictions: Smoking outdoors only. Pets are welcome, but must not be left unattended.

Situated in the Trinity National Forest on 17 forested acres, at the north end of Trinity Lake, our units offer living comfort with peace, quiet and privacy surrounded by fir, pine, and cedar trees. We have one and two bedroom cabins, the largest is 1000 sq. ft. and can sleep up to eight people.

While Enright Gulch is located on a private road off Hwy. 3, it is within a five-mile radius of grocery stores, gas stations, restaurants, laundromats, tennis courts, gift shops, and marinas and within an easy drive to numerous Trinity Alps Wilderness trailheads. For the fisherman, the Carville Dredger Pond, which is stocked with fish yearly, is within walking distance as is a swimming and fishing hole in the Trinity River.

Visitors to the area can enjoy a variety of activities. Trinity Lake offers great swimming and fishing, and local marinas have patio and smaller boats for rent as well as slips or mooring buoys for those with their own boats. There are numerous trails for hiking and backpacking into the Trinity Alps and many mountain lakes where one can drop a fishing line. Also to be enjoyed are tennis, gold panning, bicycling, bird-watching, wildflower hunting, or just relaxing in a serene environment with a good book.

Mt. Shasta Cabins & Cottages

P.O. Box 771
Mt. Shasta, CA 96067
(530) 926-5396
Owner: John Hunt

Accommodations: Cabins & cottages.

Amenities: Some with fully equipped kitchens, linens, TV, telephones, and BBQ's.

Rates: $35.00 - $295.00 per night.

Minimum Stay: One night.

Restrictions: Pets allowed in some cottages.

Mt. Shasta Cabins offers vacation lodging in and around the Mt. Shasta area. Most of our units have stocked kitchens, linens, telephones, cable TV, BBQ's, woodstoves (with wood provided), and, of course, privacy.

Our rates vary from mid-season to off-season. They also vary according to cottage size and number of persons staying.

53

This area is a wonderland of lakes, streams, and trails. There are many sites to see and things to do such as swimming, fishing, hunting, skiing, golfing, hiking, and biking.

Mt. Shasta is a beautiful mountain community nestled at the foot of the 14,162 ft. Mt. Shasta peak. The town is filled with delightful restaurants, lots of shopping, and local special events.

Pine-Gri-La

P.O. Box 100
Castella, CA 96017
(530) 235-4466
Owner: John Powell

Accommodations: 3 private and comfortable cabins.

Amenities: Peace and quiet, beauty, and a relaxed atmosphere.

Rates: $60.00 per person (includes all meals).

Minimum Stay: Two nights.

Restrictions: "It's for happy people."

Pine-gri-la is not just another lodge along the highway. It is a mountain oasis of peace and beauty. You'll find no neon, only the radiance of a rainbow's end.

Pine-gri-la is refreshing to the soul. We call it the "magic" of Pine-gri-la because we aren't quite capable of describing the soothing effects. It's not hip, Zen, religious or New Age, but it is undeniably spiritually fulfilling. Let me relate my own "conversion".

For many years, I chose not to Pine-gri-la. I was young and had to see so many cities.

Beth and I spent plenty of time enjoying Pine-gri-la but I heard the cities calling. I also heard, but never surrendered to, the forest singing. Others listened...but we played Bob Dylan, traveled and worked. We saved our money.

Several years ago, after buying out our partner Ed, we spent yet another summer at Pine-gri-la. We worked hard, spent all of our savings, and watched years of neglect blossom. The next year we did the same, and the next year we did the same.

We saw our efforts begin to reflect the natural beauty of Pine-gri-la. Once again, we heard Pine-gri-la sing. This time we listened.

We still play Bob Dylan, but we've also learned to love the natural opera of the forest: the melody of the wind in the trees, the industrious grunts of chipmunks, squirrels, and hummingbirds, and the sight and silence of a pine cone falling and a jumbo jet steady on its way.

We have learned how to Pine-gri-la.

We reopened Pine-gri-la so that everyone can listen to the forest sing. It's our obligation to share and preserve what no one can own, the simple beauty of nature and the love that it engenders.

Come up for a weekend or mid-week. Typically, the weather is gorgeous and our surroundings have Yosemite beauty without the crowds.

Sandy Bar Ranch

P.O. Box 347
Orleans, CA 95556
(530) 627-3379
(530) 627-3880 FAX
e-mail: sandybar@pcweb.net
www.pcweb.net/sandybar
Owner: Blythe Reis

Accommodations: 4 redwood cabins, all with full kitchens, separate bedroom with queen-sized bed, bathroom with shower, and outdoor deck looking onto the river. Each cabin sleeps four; additional roll-aways are available.

Amenities: Great river view and direct river access from cabin; deep swimming hole and sandy beach, whitewater rafting trips available, fresh organic produce available in season from the garden.

Rates: $68.00 for 2 people/night. $10.00/extra person over 12 years, $5.00 for kids 12 and under. Open all year.

Minimum Stay: Two nights.

Restrictions: No smoking inside cabins. Pets are welcome.

Once a Native American settlement, Sandy Bar Ranch is nestled in a beautiful valley carved out by the Klamath River in the heart of Six Rivers National Forest. Our four redwood cabins are along the river providing views of a variety of wildlife from blue herons to bald eagles, river otter to deer.

We are located in Orleans, a small former gold mining town which is home to a diverse community including Karuk people, organic farmers, artisans, miners, forest workers and Forest Service personnel. At the ranch, you'll find handmade crafts, an organic fruit and nut tree nursery and an organic flower and vegetable garden. Ask for a tour or try your hand at gardening.

Orleans is the home of both the Six Rivers and the Klamath National Forest Ranger Stations, which offer guidebooks and maps to hiking, bicycling, and other outdoor recreational activities in the area.

Both the Klamath and nearby Salmon River offer stretches of sandy beach and idyllic swimming holes. All levels of paddle or excursion rafting trips are available, ranging from mild scenic tours to daredevil whitewater.

Traditionally, some of the finest steelhead fishing in Northern California is found here. For the fungal fanatic, wild forest mushrooms abound in both spring and fall. We offer seasonal workshops in identification and cultivation with experts in the field.

Throughout the year we offer seminars focusing on the ecology of the Klamath Mountains. Call to receive our newsletter or check out our website. Sandy Bar offers an out-of-the-way retreat for exploring one of the few remaining wild areas in California.

Trinity Canyon Lodge

P.O. Box 51
Helena, CA 96048
(530) 623-6318
Owners: Joe & Diane Mercier

Accommodations: Cabins, suites, and rooms.

Amenities: River frontage. Full kitchens, carpets, colored T.V., electric or gas heat, and fully furnished. Maid service and security available.

Rates: $38.00 - $118.00 per night.

Minimum Stay: Three nights.

Restrictions: Pets okay ($5.00 charge per night). Deposits required.

Situated in the heart of Shasta-Trinity National Forest on the banks of the Trinity River, Trinity Canyon Lodge is ideally located for those seeking Northern California's finest outdoor recreation.

Find solitude and enjoy the crystal clear waters of the Trinity River and its tributaries. Swim in secluded pools. Fish the diverse year-round fishery for Salmon, Trout and Steelhead. Canoe, kayak, raft or try a relaxing tube float down the Trinity River. The lodge is located mid-way between two major trailheads into the Trinity Alps Wilderness Area for unlimited hiking. Mountain bike the extensive Forest Service road systems for adventure and exercise. Explore nearby historic locales dating from the California Gold Rush.

Visit ancient Native American villages, archaeological sites, museums and exhibits. Experience exceptional bird watching, wildlife observation and photo opportunities. Pan for gold, pick wild blackberries or simply relax with a good book by the river on our grassy beach. Directions and further information are available at Trinity Canyon Lodge for all of the above activities.

Professionally guided activities available by reservation include fishing trips, flyfishing instruction, horse pack trips into the Trinity Alps, white water rafting and environmentally oriented ecotours.

Tsasdi Resort

19990 Lakeshore Dr.
Lakehead, CA 96051
(530) 238-2575
(800) 995-0291
Your Hosts: Chuck & Bonnie Walls

Accommodations: 20 fully equipped housekeeping cabins.

Amenities: Heated pool, private dock, TV's, volleyball, basketball, game room and store. All have private decks and barbecues. Some have refrigerators.

Rates: $80.00 - $165.00 (in season). $45.00 - $100.00 (off season).

Minimum Stay: None.

Restrictions: None.

Nestled in a forest of Black Oaks overlooking beautiful Shasta Lake, Tsasdi Resort offers 20 separate, air-conditioned cabins designed with one, two or three bedrooms. Comfort and convenience are assured with the complete kitchen, shower and patio deck with picnic table. Linens, utensils, dishes and microwaves are all included to make your stay absolutely trouble-free.

Tsasdi Resort is your headquarters for discovering the scenic wonders of Northern California no matter what season you decide to play. Ski, fish, swim and boat within the 370 miles of shoreline at beautiful Shasta Lake. Explore the natural hidden beauty of Shasta Caverns and the horseshoe-shaped Burney Falls. Hike or ski Mt. Shasta's magnificent slopes and the volcano, Mt. Lassen, which last erupted 70 years ago. Hike or climb the incredible Castle Craigs.

Free boat slips are available when you stay with us, so bring your boat, or if you prefer, we can arrange a boat rental for you. Launching ramps, gas, and services are all nearby.

Enjoy the view at sunset overlooking Shasta Lake as you tend the fine art of barbecuing steaks and burgers. Share the excitement as your child battles their first Rainbow Trout or bass. Unwind as you take to your feet in this "waterskier's paradise." This is Tsasdi Resort.

NORTHERN COAST

T. THOMPSON

Emandal: A Farm on A River

16500 Hearst Road
Willits, CA 95490
(707) 459-5439
(707) 459-1808 FAX
Owners: Clive & Tamara Adams

Accommodations: Cabins with electricity, cold water, bedding, and quilts.

Amenities: River swimming, organic vegetables, fresh bread, and hammocks.

Rates: $84.00 - $97.00 per night.

Minimum Stay: Two nights.

Restrictions: No smoking. No pets.

Emandal is located 16 miles off Hwy. 101, northeast of Willits in Mendocino County, approximately 140 miles north of San Francisco, at the end of a country road. We are 60 miles from the coast and two miles from the base of San Hedrin Mountain, one of the highest points in the Coast Range. Our elevation is 1350 feet and the temperature normally registers 85-95 degrees during the summer.

There are 17 redwood cabins on the oak and fir clad hills, built by Al Byrnes between 1915 and 1925. Each cabin is furnished with beds (along with bed linen and blankets), cold spring water and electricity. A hammock is generally found close by. Bathrooms and shower facilities are located in the camp area. We serve three meals a day and there is no bar. The price for a one week stay, Sunday to Sunday, includes both the room and three meals.

Believing that families truly need time to be together in an unstructured, unpressured environment, we provide no planned activities. The Eel River borders the ranch for three miles, offering all types of swimming, driftwood gathering, rock hunting, or sunbathing. There are numerous hiking trails throughout the 1000 acres of wooded hillside. And, should you want to, there are farm chores to be done... from berry picking to egg gathering. At night, the sky offers a brilliant display of summer constellations. The camp-fire circle has held people captive for hours, with songs, stories, skits and games. Whatever you do, it's your time to do as you wish.

Fairwinds Farm B&B Cottage

P.O. Box 581
Inverness, CA 94937
(415) 663-9454
e-mail: fairwind@svn.net
Owner: Joyce Goldfield

Accommodations: One large (1000 sq ft.) cottage with queen bed downstairs, and a loft bedroom with doublebed. Also available is a cozy wing off the main house called *Dan's en suite room*.

Amenities: Fireplace, hot tub, TV/VCR & movies, stereo, direct access to 75,000 acre national seashore, barnyard animals, child's playhouse, garden with swing, ponds, and waterfalls.

Rates: $135.00 for two, $25.00 each additional person plus tax. Stay six days and get the seventh day free. *Dan's en suite room* $91.00/night for two.

Minimum Stay: Two night minimum on Friday and Saturday. One night minimum all other days.

Restrictions: No pets. Smoking outside. Children are welcome!

This is the ultimate getaway. It sits high atop Inverness Ridge, amidst towering Bishop pines and bays, with direct access to the 68,000 acres of the Point Reyes National Seashore.

The Fairwinds Farm is about an hour north of San Francisco on the Point Reyes Peninsula, an enchanting land of varied delights and topography. Explore long stretches of ocean beaches, some with heavy surf. Or, if you prefer, there are many quiet coves and secluded beaches along Tomales Bay.

Meadows of spectacular wildflowers await the hiker and photographer. Or enjoy the breathtaking views from forested mountain tops, where you may catch a glimpse of deer, fox, bobcat, possum, squirrel, rabbits, raccoons, and chipmunks. Whale watching is at its peak from December through April. The marshlands of Tomales Bay are a birdwatcher's paradise year round.

Our cottage offers a large living room, fireplace, fully equipped kitchen, bath, private garden with pond and swing, and deck-top tub with ocean view. A generous country breakfast is provided with fresh fruit, gourmet coffee and tea, homemade baked goodies, jams and molded butter. And for your evenings by the fire, special cookies, popcorn and chocolate bars, good books, soft music, and plenty of dry firewood.

Quaint, rustic, and cozy. A very special hide-a-way, secluded and private where you sleep under down comforters, lulled by owl songs. The only light visible from the farm is the lighthouse on the Farallon Islands. This is the perfect vacation spot. You need never use your car while you're here!

The Gallery Cottage

P.O. Box 118
Pt. Reyes Station, CA 94956
(415) 663-1419
Owners: Ralph & Martha Borge

Accommodations: One cottage with kitchenette.

Amenities: Woodstove, queen bed, deck, privacy, games, cable TV, and close to Pt. Reyes National Seashore.

Rates: $105.00 per night.

Minimum Stay: One night.

Restrictions: No smoking. No pets.

The hamlet of Point Reyes Station lies amid rolling pastureland near the southern tip of Tomales Bay, one mile east of Point Reyes National Seashore. On the edge of town you will find The Gallery Cottage, a guest house to the 1903 resident/art gallery of Ralph and Martha Borge. The cottage overlooks an idyllic rural setting. In the immediate foreground is a wildlife reserve, behind that the calm waters of Paper Mill Creek, and further to the west the sweeping, green expanse of Inverness Ridge.

The cottage is ideal for couples wanting a peaceful, romantic, private retreat. Guests have described it as "magical." It is charming, clean and comfortable, complete with a queen bed, couch, and wood-burning stove in one room, a bathroom with shower, a full kitchenette, and a private deck.

A breakfast is not provided, however, the kitchen comes with staples such as freshly ground coffee, decaf, and teas. Your breakfast could include a sampling of delectable pastries brought back from the nearby Cafe Reyes or the Bovine Bakery, or you may opt for a fuller gourmet breakfast at the Station House Cafe, located just one block away. If you prefer to prepare meals in the cottage, Point Reyes Station boasts of one of the largest country stores in Northern California, the Palace Food Market, an ideal place in which to stock up for a private feast. As for dining out, choices abound. Taqueria La Quinta serves fast, fresh Mexican food and is just a short walk from the cottage. The aforementioned Station House Cafe has been favorably reviewed in Gourmet Magazine.

The owners of the cottage are nationally recognized painters willing to share their art and a corner of their lives. They are always happy to point out some of the local attractions, including where to bike, hike, swim, fish, sail, horseback ride, and watch for birds and whales. If all of that sounds too hectic, feel free to sit back in peaceful seclusion or enjoy the scenery and quiet charms of this small, friendly western-style town with its gathering of art galleries and quaint shops.

Holly Tree Inn and Cottages

P.O. Box 642
Pt. Reyes Station, CA 94956
(415) 663-1554
(415) 663-8566 FAX
(800) 286-4655
Owners: Diane & Tom Balogh

Accommodations: 4 guest rooms and and 3 private cottages.

Amenities: Fireplaces and hot tubs.

Rates: $120.00 - $250.00 per night.

Minimum Stay: Two nights on weekends. One night all other times.

Restrictions: No smoking indoors.

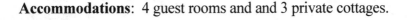

Only one hour north of San Francisco in the heart of the Point Reyes National Seashore, this enchanting country inn is nestled near a brook in a nineteen acre coastal valley of lawns, gardens, and wooded hillsides. Central to the inn are the spacious living and dining rooms decorated in country prints and antiques, with comfortable couches, French doors, and fireplaces. Four romantic guest rooms have king or queen beds and private baths.

One room has a fireplace. A full country breakfast is served before the curved hearth.

The Cottage in the Woods is a magical two room getaway with fireplace, pearwood antiques, and king size bed with crisp blue and white linens, with a sitting room, and wood-burning stove. There is a luxurious clawfoot tub in front of a greenhouse window and a separate shower. A breakfast basket is left daily. This cottage can accommodate two adults and two children on futons.

Vision Cottage, overlooking the summit of Mt. Vision, is a two bedroom cottage with full kitchen, bath, fireplace, and decks. You can hike 1.5 miles from your door along a trail to Tomales Bay. A private outdoor hot tub is available.

See also "Sea Star Cottage" (Page 103).

"Can you imagine meeting up with elk with antlers so tall that they practically poke holes in the clouds? Or standing at a lighthouse and spotting dozens of whales blowing their spouts? Or hiking to a rare waterfall that actually pours over an ocean bluff and into the sea? Or what of canoeing in quiet lagoons, walking on an earthquake fault, or combing miles of untouched beach, secret tidepools and strange sea tunnels and rock stacks set along a wilderness coastal trail? The only place on earth where these visions come true is at Point Reyes National Seashore..." (S.F. Examiner). The Inn is close to hiking, beaches, spectacular birding, wildlife, and whale viewing. Bike and horse rentals are also nearby. Your stay at the Holly Tree Inn will be a memorable one!

Horseshoe Farm Vacation Cabin

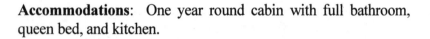

P.O. Box 332
Pt. Reyes Station, CA 94956
(415) 663-9401
e-mail: hfc@svn.net
www.horseshoefarmcabin.com
Owner: Paki Wright

Accommodations: One year round cabin with full bathroom, queen bed, and kitchen.

Amenities: Fireplace, hot tub, great views, maximum privacy, walk to hiking trails of the Point Reyes National Seashore.

Rates: $150.00 - $165.00 per night plus 10% tax.

Minimum Stay: Two night minimum stay midweek and weekends.

Restrictions: No pets. No smoking.

Horseshoe Farm Cabin is adjacent to the Pt. Reyes National Seashore, a breathtaking federal park of some 65,000 acres of beaches, mountains, meadows, and waterfalls one hour from the Golden Gate Bridge. Year round bird watching, art galleries, great restaurants and mouth-watering bakeries are in the nearby villages of Inverness and historic Point Reyes Station. The famous Pt. Reyes Lighthouse is one of the best sites on the coast of California to watch the annual gray whale migration from January to June.

Horseshoe Farm Cabin is on the edge of a large central sunny meadow in which deer frolic and through which birds soar. Secluded and high up in the evergreen woods of Inverness Ridge, Horseshoe Farm offers several acres of peace and quiet, moon and sunlight over forested canyons.

In the cabin, a cozy nest of a bedroom with queen platform bed looks out on sun-dappled woods. Full kitchen, living room with queen futon couch, fireplace/woodstove, and wood is provided. There is a sunny deck with large private spa and lovely mountain meadow view.

The unspoiled beauty of the land and beaches of West Marin, Tomales Bay, and its quaint little villages await the nature lover who is looking for a place to take a "green cure" from the rigors of our all-too-modern civilization.

Howard Creek Ranch

P.O. Box 121
Westport, CA 95488
(707) 964-6725, (707) 964-1603 FAX
www.howardcreekranch.com
Owners: Charles & Sally Grigg

Accommodations: 4 cabins, 4 suites, and 6 rooms.

Amenities: Large comfortable beds, full ranch breakfast, antiques, wood stoves, hot tub, sauna, massage, private baths, three-mile long beach, creek, views of ocean, mountain and meadow.

Rates: $75.00 - $160.00 per night.

Minimum Stay: Two nights (some weekends).

Restrictions: Smoking outdoors only.

Howard Creek Ranch is a forty acre valley on the Pacific Ocean near the "Lost Coast," a designated wilderness. The scenery is alive with the rural splendor of sweeping ocean and mountain views.

An historic 1871 farmhouse sits in the middle of this idyllic landscape with green lawns and an award-winning flower garden.

Horses, cows, sheep, a llama and a goat graze the pastures.

The ranch was first settled in 1867 as a land grant of thousands of acres and is a designated historic site. It included a sheep and cattle ranch, sawmill, a blacksmith shop, and a dairy. The buildings were constructed of virgin redwood from the ranch forest.

The inn is furnished with antiques, collectibles and memorabilia. The original fireplace still warms the parlour. A 75-foot swinging footbridge spans Howard Creek as it flows past barns and outbuildings to the beach 200 yards away.

Breakfast features souffles, sausage or bacon, buttermilk pancakes with bananas, blackberries or raspberries, baked apples with granola, fresh fruit and juice, hot coffee and teas, or similar yummy menus.

"Of the dozen or so inns on the West Coast we have visited, this is easily the most enchanting one," California Magazine.

Details: Suites and cabins, hot tub, sauna, massage by reservation, private/shared bath, views of the ocean, mountains, meadows, creek, fireplaces/wood stoves, plentiful books, fresh flowers, and good conversation. Gift certificates are available. Activities on the coast range from horseback riding, hiking and deep-sea fishing, to shopping and cultural events.

"This is one of the most romantic places on the planet", San Francisco Examiner.

The Inn at Schoolhouse Creek

N. Hwy. 1, P.O. Box 1637
Mendocino, CA 95460
(707) 937-5525, (800) 731-5525
www.schoolhousecreek.com
Owners: Al & Penny Greenwood

Accommodations: 4 lodge rooms, 9 cottages and 2 luxury suites.

Amenities: Fireplaces, decks, some kitchens, breakfast, ocean view hot tub, and ocean access.

Rates: $115.00 - 210.00 per night (weekend and summer rates), slightly lower rates available off season Sunday - Thursday.

Minimum Stay: Two nights on weekends. Three nights on major holidays.

Restrictions: No smoking. Pets permitted in some units.

Facing the Pacific Ocean like a small, rural community, the Inn at Schoolhouse Creek has offered lodging to coastal visitors since the 1930's. Separate cottages and rooms in small buildings all have ocean views, fireplaces, and private baths. Many have spa tubs.

Located on eight acres of flowering gardens, meadow and forest, the Inn was once part of a large coastal ranch and still reminds you of earlier times.

The lovely old Ledford home, built in 1862, serves as a comfortable meeting area where guests can curl up by the fireplace with a book or game. Breakfast is served on the sun porch and evening hors d'oeuvres are enjoyed in the library.

The cottages were built at the turn of the century. All have fireplaces, some have kitchens, decks, and wonderful ocean views. Four other more contemporary rooms offer the spaciousness of redwood beam ceilings, fireplaces, ocean views, and small decks. Two luxury suites have commanding views and feature king beds, whirlpool tubs, and fireplaces.

The charming and historic village of Mendocino, with its many fine galleries and shops, is only three miles away. The surrounding area offers rivers, harbors, beaches, and spectacular state parks, as well as wine tasting in the nearby Anderson Valley.

The Inn offers a relaxed and comfortable atmosphere where you can enjoy your vacation on your own schedule. Sit in the gardens, watch the waves break and whales spout; walk among the ferns and giant cypress at Schoolhouse Creek, and watch the deer browse in the meadow. The sense of quiet and peace of this country environment is relaxation at its best.

Jasmine Cottage & Gray's Retreat

P.O. Box 56
Pt. Reyes Station, CA 94956
(415) 663-1166
(415) 663-9565 FAX
Owner: Karen Gray

Accommodations: Two cottages.

Amenities: Full kitchens, fireplaces, garden hot tub, naturalists' libraries, secluded gardens, porta-crib, and high chair.

Rates: $115.00 per night for two, $15.00 each additional person; weekly rate of $700.00.

Minimum Stay: One night during the week. Two nights on the weekend.

Restrictions: No smoking inside. Inquire about pets.

Jasmine Cottage and Gray's Retreat share the grounds with the original Point Reyes Schoolhouse (now the proprietor's home) on the hill above the western farming town of Point Reyes Station. The cottages are just five minutes by car from the headquarters for the magnificent Point Reyes National Seashore, and just a five minute walk down the hill to town.

Jasmine Cottage, set in a secluded garden, is a cozy cottage with two twin beds, one queen, full kitchen, shower and bath, woodstove, and a large naturalists' library. Country floral furnishings of wood and wicker were chosen for comfort as well as charm.

Gray's Retreat is farthest back on the property with beautiful views of the grassy meadow and Inverness Ridge sunsets. The retreat is a rustic cedar barn with all the luxuries of today: full kitchen with gas stove, dishwasher, microwave, gas wall-heaters, view skylights, full bath, Franklin fireplace, BBQ, and two furnished patios for six. The Retreat sleeps six with a four-poster queen in the bedroom, a sofabed double, and a trundle double in the living area. The dining table seats eight nicely. French doors lead out from all rooms onto the garden patios. Furnishings are wood and wicker. A good naturalists' library is housed in the living room.

The two places share a secluded hot tub area hidden in the gardens between them. Guests use the spa on a first come first serve basis simply locking the garden gate and throwing a towel over the trellis to signal that the spa is in use. There is a shared laundry, telephone, and television by request. The children's playground is just across the road.

These cottages offer the peace and quiet of the country just above town. Thousands of acres of National Seashore and woodlands await the hiker, bird watcher, whale watcher, and naturalist all times of the year.

Jim's Soda Bay Resort

6380 Soda Bay Rd.
Kelseyville, CA 95451
(707) 279-4837
Owners: Jim & Rose McLaughlin

Accommodations: 5 cottages with full kitchens, living/sleeping room plus separate bedroom and bathroom.

Amenities: TV's, kitchens are fully equipped with cooking and eating utensils. Bedding and towels are provided. Each unit has a patio with table and BBQ grill. Units are air-conditioned. Free boat launching and boat slip for guests.

Rates: $45.00 - $55.00 per night.

Minimum Stay: None.

Restrictions: Small pets are sometimes allowed with leash. Call for these restrictions.

Jim's Soda Bay Resort is a small resort located on the Soda Bay inlet on the south shore of Clear Lake, 4 miles north of Kelseyville and 9 miles south of Lakeport.

The resort is small, family-owned and operated, with nice cabins, a boat dock, launching ramp, small beach, and swimming area. These are for the exclusive use of Jim's and Rose's guests along with a large lawn area for sunbathing.

Cabin #2 has a bedroom with a queen bed, a living/sleeping area with a double bed, and a porch with a nice view of the lake.

Cabin #3 has a queen bed in the bedroom, the living/sleeping area has a double bed plus a single day bed. This unit has a patio.

Cabin #4 has a bedroom with a queen bed, a living/sleeping area with 2 double beds plus a porch with a view of the lake.

Cabin #5 has a bedroom with a queen bed, a living/sleeping area with a double bed, and a double hide-a-bed.

Unit #9 is a mobilehome with a bedroom and queen bed, a separate living room with a double hide-a-bed, and a separate kitchen area.

Lawsons' Resort

P.O. Box 97
Dillon Beach, CA 94929
(707) 878-2204
(707) 878-2505 FAX
Owners: The Lawson Family

Accommodations: Cottages and vacation rental homes.

Amenities: TV/VCR, fully equipped kitchens, panoramic ocean views, woodstoves, and a safe swimming beach.

Rates: $250.00 per weekend; $740.00 per week.

Minimum Stay: One night.

Restrictions: No smoking. No pets.

Lawsons' Resort overlooks Tomales Bay and the Pacific Ocean in the picturesque village of Dillon Beach located four miles west of Hwy. 1 at the town of Tomales.

Enjoy our beautiful swimming beach. Peek into its tide pools or surf fish and poke pole along the rocky cliffs, catching eel, sea trout, cabezoni, and blue cod. Rock or surf fish along the beach, using your surf casting rod to catch redtail or rubberlip perch or striped bass. Hike or lounge in towering sand dunes.

Picnic tables and BBQ's are provided on the beach. Facilities for large groups are available by reservation.

Exciting ocean waves provide fun and thrills for surfing, boogie boarding, jet skiing, windsurfing, and skim boarding. Boogie board rentals are at Lawsons' Store. Clamming, salmon fishing, and charter boats are a mile away.

Lawsons' Store carries a complete line of groceries, beer, wine, and all your camping and fishing supplies. We also carry a large line of kites and accessories. The Treasure Cove Gift Shop has jewelry, sea shells, T-shirts, and novelties.

Marsh Cottage Bed & Breakfast

P.O. Box 1121
Pt. Reyes Station, CA 94956
(415) 669-7168
www.marshcottage.com
Owner: Wendy Schwartz

Accommodations: One cottage with queen & twin bed.

Amenities: Full private bath, full kitchen, fireplace, decks, and spectacular views of bay and mountains.

Rates: $150.00 per night. Weekly rate is available.

Minimum Stay: Two nights on weekends and holidays.

Restrictions: No smoking. No pets.

Located one mile from Inverness and near the Point Reyes National Seashore, Marsh Cottage has been a favorite retreat since 1985 for those who prefer the comforts of a bed and breakfast in the privacy of their own completely equipped cottage. Only one party of two (or three - and, children are welcome) can occupy Marsh Cottage at one time; there are no other units. The cottage sits on a salt/freshwater marsh along Tomales Bay -- local wildlife and flora create a unique and magical setting that enhances guests' experience of the Point Reyes area in all its seasons. It has a full kitchen, bath, queen bed, desk and sitting area, fireplace, guidebooks, daypacks, board games, even binoculars. Breakfast is provided in the privacy of the cottage, and consists of fresh orange juice, muffins or breakfast bread, fresh fruits in season, milk and granola cereals, local cheese, a basket of eggs, and a generous assortment of teas, and regular and decaf french roast coffee. You may choose to take breakfast out on the sunny deck overlooking the bay and Black Mountain.

Originally built in the 30's, its style is that of a nostalgic Cape Cod country cottage -- with grey wood exterior, white trim, remodeled white wood interior, mullioned (small paned) windows, colors of teal, white, beige, terracotta on coordinated print fabrics, practical antiques, front porch and deck with furnishings.

A perfect base from which to explore spectacular Point Reyes National Seashore as well as Tomales Bay State Park, with its miles of trails in every type of scenic terrain, prolific wildlife, private coves and dramatic beaches all accessible by car, foot, bike, or horseback. Both the enchanting Inverness and classically western Point Reyes Station are close by hosting a variety of good restaurants and shops both practical and unique. Begin your adventures at the Bear Valley Visitors Center, or use one of the many guidebooks in the cottage, for a day of hiking, tidepooling, winter whale-watching, bird watching, picnicking, swimming, exploring hillsides of wildflowers, or, like many guests, just linger in the magical setting of Marsh Cottage.

Mar Vista Cottages at Anchor Bay

35101 South Hwy 1
Gualala, CA 95445
(707) 884-3522, (707) 884-4861 FAX
toll free (877) 855-3522
e-mail: renata@marvistamendocino.com
www.MarVistaMendocino.com
Owners: Renata & Tom Dorn

Accommodations: 12 Housekeeping Cottages (8 one bedroom and 4 two bedroom).

Amenities: Kitchens, linens, barbecues, fire pit, fireplaces, picnic tables, Japanese soaking tub, ocean views, decks, hiking, horseback riding, bicycling, golf, boating, kayaking, canoeing, fishing, excellent restaurants and much more.

Rates: $115.00 - $135.00 (one bedroom cottages); $145.00 - $155.00 (two bedroom cottages).

Minimum Stay: Two nights on the weekend.

Restrictions: No smoking in cottages. Eight day cancellation.

Mar Vista Cottages are reminders of a simpler life. Owners Renata and Tom Dorn believe in what they call "comfort lodging". That is a little like mashed potatoes – it is familiar and uncomplicated, an environment where one can feel completely at ease. Comfort lodging is very satisfying and still affordable.

Mar Vista happily welcomes children and pets. The interiors are designed specifically to favor special guests while still maintaining the highest housekeeping standards. The cottages are uncluttered and without fuss, with hardwood floors, country furniture, lots of slipcovers and maximum storage opportunities like miles of peg rail for everyone's paraphernalia.

The cottages were built in the 1930's as fishing cabins. Twelve cottages sit in a horseshoe pattern on nine acres of gently sloping hillside looking out at the Pacific Ocean. It feels like summer camp with forests of Redwood and Douglas Fir surrounding the cottages like an embrace. The central meadow has old stone grills, picnic tables and a fire pit.

There is a redwood soaking tub under a gazebo by two ponds in the meadow – a favorite soaking time is when the moon is full and shimmering on the ocean. The most unusual and delightful experience for guests at Mar Vista will be the Permaculture Garden and Orchard, a demonstration project for sustainable living in progress. Guests may collect just laid eggs, fruit, vegetables, herbs and flowers to take back to their cottage kitchens.

Comforts never cease. There is the secluded and sheltered Fish Rock Gulch Beach just steps away, or the quiet trail down through the redwoods to Ferguson Creek. There are the wondrous sounds of the ocean's roar, the barking sea lions, and the rippling creek water outside your bedroom window

Mattole River Resort

42354 Mattole Rd.
Petrolia, CA 95558
(707) 629-3445
(800) 845-4607
Owner: Steve Bowser

Accommodations: 6 cabins all with kitchens.

Amenities: River swimming, beach hiking, conservation area, hiking or biking.

Rates: $35.00 - $90.00 per night.

Minimum Stay: One night.

Restrictions: None.

Some of California's most rugged and majestic land is on the Lost Coast of Humboldt County, a remote area untouched by major highways or towns. It extends from just south of Ferndale to northern Mendocino county. Much of the land lies within the King Range National Conservation Area, a mountain wilderness and coastline of haunting beauty. Seals, sea lions and marine birds live here, as well as elk, bald eagles, spotted owls, black bear, and black tailed deer.

In the heart of the Lost Coast region is the Mattole River Resort, a colony of fully equipped cabins with kitchenettes, some of which can hold up to six adults. There are facilities also for campers amid the shade trees. We are located on the two-lane county road between Honeydew and Petrolia described in *California* magazine as *"...the quintessential Sunday drive; pastoral, scenic, good for top speeds of 35 mph. It follows the loopy, north-flowing Mattole, a splendid green angling stream..."*

Since the nearest urban area is about 60 miles from here, guests can enjoy a magnificently starry night sky without distracting artificial lights.

During the winter and early spring, fishermen prize the Mattole River, described by the California Department of Fish and Game as *"one of the finest steelhead fishing streams on the North Coast"*.

In the warm months visitors swim in the river and bicycle on the local roads. The really adventuresome may enjoy hiking the 24 miles of unspoiled ocean beach in the King Range Wilderness, or climbing to the summit of 4000′ King's Peak. Arrangements can be made for resort staff to shuttle you to the trailheads. We also have mountain and road bikes to rent by the day.

Murphy's Jenner Inn & Cottages

P.O. Box 69
Jenner, CA 95450
(707) 865-2377
(707) 865-0829 FAX
Owners: Richard & Sheldon Murphy
Innkeeper: Jenny Carroll

Accommodations: Bed & Breakfast: 4 cottages, 3 suites, and 6 rooms.

Vacation Rentals: 6 homes.

Amenities: All B&B accommodations with private bathrooms and separate entrances, and most have private decks with water views. Fireplaces, kitchens and hot tubs available.

Rates: Rooms: $65.00 - $108.00; Suites & Cottages: $118.00 - $165.00; Vacation Homes: $150.00 - $225.00. Weekly rates available for all accommodations.

Minimum Stay: Two nights on weekends. Three nights on holiday weekends.

Restrictions: No pets. Smoking outdoors only.

On the undiscovered Sonoma Coast between Pt. Reyes National

Seashore and Ft. Bragg, the tiny village of Jenner-By-The-Sea nestles in the hills where the beautiful Russian River meets the Pacific Ocean. Murphy's Jenner Inn offers warm hospitality and cozy bed and breakfast accommodations in a collection of traditional seaside cottages.

Three large cottages have suites with fireplaces and kitchenettes, plus 2 or 3 additional private rooms. Four smaller cottages are individual little hideaways. Lovingly decorated with antiques, wicker, houseplants, and unique touches, each has a distinct character and personality.

The heart of the Inn is it's lodge parlor, where guests gather for breakfast, and drop in to enjoy teas and aperitifs by the fire in the afternoons and evenings. Fine dining is provided by the Jenner-By-The-Sea Restaurant next door. The Jenner Inn also offers private vacation homes with spectacular panoramic views of the ocean, beach, and river.

Jenner is a refuge for coastal wildlife. A boat launch into the river's estuary allows kayaks, canoes, and small sailboats to glide gently out for an up-close view of the harbor seals, river otters, and hundreds of varieties of water fowl. Fifteen miles of sandy beaches and state parks surround the village.

Jenner is also an ideal "home base" for exploring many of Northern California's wonders. There are miles of hiking and bicycling trails. We invite you to experience Jenner-By-The-Sea, a quiet, protected village blessed with the warmest weather on the North Coast and a setting of exceptional beauty and tranquility.

The Narrows Lodge Resort

5690 Blue Lakes Rd.
Upper Lake, CA 95485
(707) 275-2718
(800) 476-2776
(707) 275-0301 FAX
Owners: Brian & Gail Ogram

Accommodations: 2 cabins with kitchens overlooking the lake; 15 motel rooms and 4 with kitchens. Coffee service is provided.

Amenities: 30 RV sites with full hookups and 9 campsites with water and electricity, day use area, picnic tables and BBQ's, beach area with lawn and trees.

Rates: $47.00 - $90.00 for rooms and cabins; $18.00 - $20.00 RV sites and campsites. Weekly rates are available.

Minimum Stay: Varies.

Restrictions: Non-smoking rooms are available.

The Narrows Lodge is located on Blue Lakes Road on the edge of Blue Lakes just off Hwy. 20, 11.5 miles east of Hwy. 101.

Bring your own boat or rent one of ours. We have row boats, motor boats, kayaks or paddle boats for rent at reasonable prices.

Fish from the dock or swim in the beautiful lake and relax by the lake on the lawn. Walking and hiking trails and bicycle riding are all available at The Narrows. Restaurants and stores are located within a 10 minute drive.

For the active vacationer there are 7 golf courses, many tennis courts, wine tasting, antiquing, off road vehicle areas, and Las Vegas style Bingo and Casino within a short distance of The Narrows. We can help you find your favorite activity in uncrowded surroundings and at reasonable prices.

North Coast Country Inn

34591 S. Hwy. 1
Gualala, CA 95445
(707) 884-4537
(800) 959-4537
Owners: Maureen and Bill Shupe

Accommodations: Full breakfast, fireplaces, private decks, hot tub, and a gazebo garden.

Rates: $160.00 to $185.00 per night.

Minimum Stay: Two nights on weekends. Three nights on holiday weekends.

Restrictions: No pets. No smoking.

Overlooking the Pacific Ocean is this cluster of restored redwood buildings with rugged shake roofs nestled into a redwood and pine forest. The hillside property that houses the bed & breakfast was once part of a coastal sheep ranch. Below the buildings is a colorful country garden with lawn, brick pathways, and fruit trees. Guest accommodations range from a private guest house with deck, fireplace, skylights, and four-poster bed to rooms with such details as French doors, fireplaces, open beam ceilings, French and European antiques and ocean view decks. All accommodations boast private baths and some have kitchenettes.

Guests at the Inn enjoy breakfast, which is served in the Common Room, and consists of a hot entree, fresh fruit, freshly baked muffins, cinnamon rolls or croissants. A freshly brewed pot of coffee is also included in the morning meal, but all guest rooms are stocked with a coffee pot, coffee, and juice. A favorite spot at the Inn is the hot tub on the hillside under towering pines with the sound of sea lions barking in the distance.

One Fifty-Five Pine

P.O. Box 62
Bolinas, CA 94924
(415) 868-0263
Owner: Karen Arthur

Accommodations: 2 cabins overlooking the ocean.

Amenities: Knotty pine cabins with big stone fireplaces and lots of windows looking out at the Pacific Ocean.

Rates: $125.00 - $135.00 per night (for two); $25.00 for each additional person. Off-season and weekly rates are available.

Minimum Stay: Two nights on the weekend.

Restrictions: No pets. Smoking outdoors only.

The two cabins at One Fifty-Five Pine are located on Duxbury Point overlooking the ocean at the southern tip of the Point Reyes National Seashore. We are about an hour north of San Francisco on the coast with westward views of the Farallone Islands and beautiful sunsets over the water. The setting is rural. The cabins are on a three acre field of wild grasses on the cliff above Agate Beach. There is a path out the backyard that winds down the hill, about a three minute walk to the beach. Agate Beach is on an intertidal reef. At low tide the tidepools are pristine. It is possible to walk for miles on the beach, or on nearby trails, or simply bring a picnic and a book and find a secluded cove to spend the day.

The cabins were built as beach cottages in the early 1950's. Each one is a small house unto itself with knotty pine interior, beam ceilings, big stone fireplace in the living room, double bed, and queen bed. There is a full kitchen and bath with tile shower, dining area, front and back deck, and lots of windows with fantastic ocean views in both cabins. One cabin has two bedrooms, the other has one bedroom.

We can offer you information about the area, discuss hiking trails, restaurants, beaches, and cabin particulars. We leave everything in the cabin for the duration of the stay. A full breakfast is provided in the kitchen. It includes muffins, fresh fruit, eggs, jam, butter, milk, cereals (hot and cold), teas and coffee beans. Charcoal for the barbecue is provided as well as firewood and kindling for the stone fireplaces. Each house has heat as well as a fireplace. We make ourselves available if anyone needs anything, although, we try to think of everything ahead of time because the cabins are very private, and self-contained retreats.

It is a very quiet, romantic area with sweeping views of the ocean and the beauty of nature surrounds us. Bordering the Point Reyes National Seashore, the village of Bolinas is a mile away. Several coastal towns are within a half hour drive.

Patrick Creek Lodge & Historical Inn

13950 Hwy. 199
Gasquet, CA 95543
(707) 457-3323
Owners: Bill & Cindy Grier

Accommodations: 10 rooms in the lodge which include 3 suites and 2 continental style rooms; 6 motel style rooms adjoining lodge; a fully self-contained, fully-furnished 2 bedroom cabin located above Patrick Creek.

Amenities: Total detachment from today's modern amenities (no phones and no TV's in rooms). Hiking and camping in the National Recreation Area plus swimming in the Smith River or the lodge pool.

Rates: $79.50 for 2 (summer rates for lodge and motel rooms); $109.50 for 2 (summer rates for 2 bedroom cabin). Winter rates are approximately 10% less.

Minimum Stay: None.

Restrictions: No pets. Limited smoking areas.

Patrick Creek Lodge's historical background ties it to the Pacific settlers during the Gold Rush Era. It's establishment is directly tied to the original toll road that passed by the lodge in the 1890's. Patrick Creek Lodge is located on Hwy. 199 between Cave Junction, Oregon, and Crescent City, California, on the famous Smith River and Patrick Creek Streams which are famous for salmon and wild steelhead. Considered the "gateway to the redwoods", Patrick Creek Lodge has nature's ambience, pioneer history, and allows it's patrons isolation from today's outside pressures.

Breakfast, lunch, and dinner is served daily with a champagne brunch served every Sunday. Full lounge service is available plus a complete wine list.

Business seminars or large outdoor weddings and reunions are welcome.

Rosemary Cottage

P.O. Box 273
Inverness, CA 94937
(415) 663-9338
Owner: Suzanne Storch

Accommodations: One cottage (other cottages also available).

Amenities: Fully furnished kitchen, large bedroom with queen bed, wood-burning stove, and additional sleeping place in the main room.

Rates: $202.00 per night with breakfast ($21.00 each additional person); $190.00 per night without breakfast ($15.00 each additional person). Off season rates available. Midweek rates available.

Minimum Stay: None.

Restrictions: Pets okay with prior arrangement. Families welcome. Crib available.

If you're longing for a secluded little paradise where you can be temporarily removed from the rest of the world, Rosemary Cottage is the place for you. A wall of windows overlooks a dramatic sylvan scene - a sunlit wooded gulch that is a sanctuary to many wild birds of the Pt. Reyes National Seashore. You lie on the deck at night and marvel at stars that never seemed so bright before. A romantic French-country cottage is your own private hideaway, luxuriate in its seclusion and the beauty surrounding it. Here you can slow down, unwind and tune in to nature. Most people leave completely refreshed. The light-flooded cottage has a high cathedral ceiling, many handcrafted details, a wood-burning stove that can be run open as a fireplace, a well-equipped kitchen and space that will comfortably sleep four.

The front wall of windows and skylight brings you close to the natural beauty of the spot even in the rain when you can witness the magical effect created as fingers of fog drift over the trees and through the canyon.

Under an old oak tree, the large deck overlooks an herb and flower garden. It is a marvelous setting for alfresco meals. The main room is comfortably furnished with antiques, oriental rugs and art. Colors of Provence, French fabrics, and personal touches create a cozy warmth. The bedroom can be closed off from the main room and includes a queen bed. The bath has a tub and shower with French tiles.

The cottage is set back through the woods from the road and the owner's house. There is a small orchard with a dozen fruit and nut trees, many 200′ Douglas Firs, and spacious old oaks.

Settle into quiet relaxation or take off to enjoy the beaches, hiking trails, and prolific wildlife of the Pt. Reyes National Seashore. Rosemary Cottage is near it all - in a world of it's own.

Sea Star Cottage

c/o Holly Tree Inn
P.O. Box 642
Pt. Reyes Station, CA
(415) 663-1554
(800) 286-4655
(415) 663-8566 FAX
Owners: Diane & Tom Balogh

Accommodations: One cottage.

Amenities: Woodburning stove, birding telescope, and hot tub.

Rates: $250.00 per night.

Minimum Stay: Two nights on weekends. One night all other times.

Restrictions: No smoking indoors. Two adults only.

Sea Star Cottage is a small rustic house built on its own pier out over the tidal waves of Tomales Bay just north of the village of Inverness. A 75-foot dock leads to the front door, which opens into a cozy living room with woodburning fireplace, couch, and comfortable rocking chair overlooking the water. It has a four poster queen size bed, blue and white tiled bathroom, a fully equipped kitchen, and solarium with hot tub. The view of the bay and wildlife are unobstructed from Hog Island to the north, to Black Mountain and Mount Tamalpais to the south.

Breakfasts are prepared in advance and await your arrival. A typical breakfast consists of fresh orange juice (there is a juicer in the kitchen), fresh fruit salad, quiche and almond croissant. Both regular coffee and freshly brewed decaffeinated coffee, as well as a selection of teas, are available. You can enjoy your breakfast in the sunny breakfast room overlooking the Inverness Yacht Club or out on the deck.

Check-in time is 5 to 7 pm Monday through Friday, and from 3 to 5 pm on Saturday and Sunday. Due to our busy schedule, preparing cottages, breakfasts, and rooms during the day, we will not be able to check you in any earlier. If your plans bring you to the area before the check-in time, visit the Bear Valley Visitors Center on Bear Valley Road. Or you can enjoy a cup of coffee at one of West Marin's bakeries: The Gray Whale in Inverness, Debra's Bakery in Inverness Park, the Bovine Bakery, or the Station House Cafe in Point Reyes Station. Please stop at the Holly Tree Inn to get the key and directions from our innkeeper. Check-out time is 11:30 am. Sea Star is a non-smoking cottage except on the outdoor decks.

Serenisea

36100 Hwy. 1 So.
Gualala, CA 95445
(707) 884-3836, (800) 331-3836
www.serenisea.com
Owner: Jim Lotter

Accommodations: Housekeeping cottages and vacation homes by or near the ocean.

Amenities: Kitchens, decks, fireplaces/woodstove, some with cable TV, hot tubs, and sandy beach access.

Rates: $85.00 - $200.00 per night.

Minimum Stay: Two nights on weekends. Cottages (one night during the week); vacation homes (two nights during the week).

Restrictions: Pets and children under 16 permitted. Smoking permitted (varies from unit to unit).

On a bluff point above the Pacific sits one of the Mendocino Coast's most intimate and beautiful small resorts -- Serenisea. Serenisea is on the legendary coast Hwy. 1, a 1½ hour - 2½ hour drive from the Bay Area and Sacramento. Facilities include housekeeping cottages located on this dramatic point, and vacation homes located in spectacular oceanfront, oceanview and redwood forest locations along our coast. Custom homes with hot tubs, stereos, cable TV, and bluff edge locations, or modest cottages with kitchens and fireplaces, in beautiful settings, show the spectrum of accommodations available.

Serenisea accommodations are ideal for romantic couples that want an ocean setting with total privacy, families who want to stay together (homes sleep from 2 - 8 people), or folks on a budget who want to save money by sharing a home with friends and splitting the cost.

Activities you can enjoy while staying in a Serenisea home range from beachcombing to skin and scuba diving, fishing, watching for whales, kayaking on the Gualala River, hiking, horseback riding, tennis at the local park, shopping, fine dining, concerts, or see a movie in one of the great old theaters anywhere. You may choose to visit historic Fort Ross, Mendocino, the wineries of the Anderson Valley, or take a trip on the "Skunk" train out of Fort Bragg.

Each season brings something different to do. In summer, there are fairs, festivals, special events, and BBQ's. Fall weather is sunny and mild, the favorite time to experience the coast. The winter is a time for storms, whales, steelhead fishing, and snuggling by a fire. Spring is when the whales return north with their babies, and wildflowers abound.

Every unit at Serenisea is unique. Some have unique art or antiques. Many are decorated in distinctive motifs. Unlike many vacation home rentals, our homes come fully equipped, including sheets and towels. Restrictions vary for each unit. Call Serenisea for our brochure which describes each home in detail.

TreeTops Cottage

43600 Little Lake Road
Mendocino, CA 95460
(707) 937-4040
Owner: Steven & Cherie Sanders

Accommodations: Cottage (one bedroom); house (3 bedroom with 2 bath).

Amenities: Kitchen, fireplace, woodburning stove, hot tub, BBQ, cable TV, VCR, tape deck, king size bed, towels, linens, and bedding.

Rates: $125.00 per night plus tax and $40.00 cleaning fee. Large house: $125.00 - $175.00 per night.

Minimum Stay: Two nights. Three nights on holidays.

Restrictions: No smoking inside. Pets okay with prior arrangement.

TreeTops Cottage is the perfect retreat for two. Located only two scenic miles from the ocean (and Mendocino), it sits on twenty-eight acres of magnificent redwood forest. Nestled among towering redwoods and wild rhododendrons, wander the grounds of what was originally known as the Paddleford Estate. Watch the deer graze in the meadow. The adventurous can hike on the trails above the fern-covered Jack Peters Gulch, or explore the forest's redwood fairy rings.

This one bedroom cottage was designed and built by David Clayton, a famous local architect, who took great care to blend TreeTops style with the environment. A beautiful, ancient Madrone tree trunk forms part of the inner stairway leading to a cozy loft. The cathedral ceilings and sixteen windows give you the comforting feeling of being nestled in your own magical tree house. Curl up on the sofa and watch the cracking fire in the brick fireplace in front of you.

TreeTops has a fully equipped kitchen with a refrigerator, stove, microwave, toaster, oven, coffee maker, dishes, large chopping block table, and dining table.

After an active day of hiking, beach combing or shopping in the village of Mendocino, complete your day by soaking in the soothing waters of your own private hot tub overlooking the beautiful redwood forest canyon and sharing the enchantment of your stay. Let Treetops Cottage be your own personal oasis.

Whispering Pines Resort

17140 Hwy. 175
Middletown, CA 95461-9738
(707) 928-5227
(707) 928-5227 FAX
www.whisperingpines.com
Owners: Madeline & Steve Strickler

Accommodations: 30 housekeeping cottages.

Amenities: Swimming pool, tennis court, basketball, volleyball, horseshoes, playground, and bike trails.

Rates: $392.00 - $441.00 per week.

Minimum Stay: Two nights.

Restrictions: No pets.

Whispering Pines Resort is an ideal family resort located between Calistoga and Clearlake on beautiful Cobb Mountain in Lake County.

Family-owned for four generations, this resort has thirty housekeeping cottages, with two and three bedrooms. Authentic log cabins are available. All cottages are spread over ten acres among pine trees. Each cottage is equipped with a complete kitchen (oven, stove, refrigerator, dishes, etc.), bathroom (shower included), and a large outside deck with table and benches. Cribs are available.

For recreation, we offer a swimming pool, tennis court, basketball and volleyball court, as well as a playground for children, bike trails, and horseshoes. Close by are two golf courses, restaurants, and churches.

This is an ideal spot for family reunions, weddings, and seminars. It's time to spend your vacation in the mountains at Whispering Pines Resort.

White Sulphur Springs Resort and Spa

3100 White Sulphur Springs
St. Helena, CA 94574
(707) 963-8588, (800) 593-8873 – CA & NV
(707) 963-2890 FAX
Owners: Buzz and Betty Foote

Accommodations: 9 small one room creekside cottages and 2 inns.

Amenities: Wine tasting, massage, facials, mud wraps, sulphur soaking pool, whirlpool bath, hiking trails and continental breakfasts.

Rates: $90.00 - $245.00 per night for 1 or 2 people.

Minimum Stay: One night in Carriage House; two nights (weekends & holidays) for inn and cottages.

Restrictions: No pets. No smoking inside. No RVs/camping.

If your idea of a getaway is a small simple creekside cottage nestled in a quiet canyon with a few walks in the woods and dips in a warm spring hot tub and pool…this idyllic spa retreat is just a couple of country miles from downtown St. Helena.

Established in 1852, White Sulphur Springs is the oldest retreat in California. It was purchased in 1983 by Buzz and Betty Foote, who have been gradually and respectfully upgrading the property with the accent on simplicity and natural beauty.

Guests can stay in three types of lodging: small one-room, Creekside Cottages with 1 or 2 queen beds, simple inn rooms with private bathrooms, or modest Carriage House rooms with shared bathrooms down the hall.

In keeping with a true getaway retreat, there are no phones or televisions in any of the rooms. Frankly, you can't help but feel at peace here – so much so that, if you're the nature-retreat type, you can remain on-site (except for jaunts into town for fine dining) and your vacation would still be fulfilling.

Commune with nature on a walk in the woods. Melt away cares with a soak in the warm sulfur spring. Lounge by the hot tub and unheated pool. Discover the simple tranquility of a shaded picnic bench. Pamper yourself with a soothing Swedish massage (indoors or outdoors for two), revitalizing Jurlique herbal facial, and relaxing body wrap.

Do what you like, but don't book a room here if you're the type who needs large luxury accommodations or special services. At White Sulphur Springs, simple pleasures are second nature.

Windmist Cottage

P.O. Box 291
Dillon Beach, CA 94929
(707) 878-2465
Owner: Charlotte Smith

Accommodations: One guest suite with private bath, sitting room, and enclosed sun porch.

Amenities: Woodstove, full breakfast, view of Pacific Ocean to the west, and a view of the coast range to the east.

Rates: $85.00 per night plus 10% tax.

Minimum Stay: One night.

Restrictions: No smoking. No pets. Children over five years old are welcome. Credit cards not accepted.

Windmist Cottage is a private passive solar home located 75 miles north of San Francisco offering a guest suite with sweeping views of the Pacific Ocean and the California Coast Range.

Accommodations include a bedroom with a queen bed and two twin beds, private bath, sitting room with woodstove, and a comfortable enclosed sun porch from which to watch local deer feeding or the sunset on the Pacific.

A full country breakfast with fresh local fruits and homemade breads is served.

Activities include beachcombing and surf fishing, or clamming, bird watching, and picnicking. Nearby Point Reyes National Seashore offers great hiking trails and whale watching. Also nearby is the world-famous California wine country which offers wine tasting, spectacular country scenes, and quaint village shopping.

Wishing Well Cottages

P.O. Box 487
Fort Bragg, CA 95437
(707) 961-5450
Owners: Kacey & Jim Davis

Accommodations: 2 cottages (1 bedroom/1 bath) with full kitchens and living rooms with sofa sleepers.

Amenities: Fireplace, cable TV, telephone, BBQ, day-use area with campfire ring, and forest walking trails.

Rates: Queen bed cottage ($70.00/night or $350.00/week); king-bed cottage: ($80.00/night or $400.00/week).

Minimum Stay: Two days.

Restrictions: Maximum of 4 people per cottage. Only well-behaved pets and children allowed.

Located on Hwy. 20 just 1 & 1/2 miles from the Pacific Ocean, the cottages sit close to the tree line of a private four acre forest that abounds with ferns, ivy, wildflowers, huckleberry, wild rhododendron, and wild mushrooms. Visit our 500 year-old redwood and peek at deer, quail, and doves in their natural setting.

Just a 5 minute drive from Noyo Harbor, 10 minutes from Fort Bragg, and 15 minutes from Mendocino, we have the perfect location for enjoying all the many sites and activities of this unique area on the California Coast.

Here are just a few of the many things to enjoy while staying at Wishing Well Cottages:

Noyo Harbor: Enjoy a working port with fish markets, seafood restaurants and dockside fish and chips. Check out the whale-watch tours, charter fishing & diving boats, scuba shop and bait/tackle store. Enjoy seals and sea lions at play and sunsets that are breathtaking.

Skunk Train: In operation since the 1850's these old steam locomotives take passengers through old stands of redwood that are not accessible by car. It is a nostalgic and educational journey into the past.

And much, much more: State Parks with scenic trails and oceanside camping, horseback rides on the beach, canoeing, bike trails, abalone diving, beachcombing, golf, tennis, wineries, breweries, museums, antique shops, art galleries, locally-made food, wine, beer and coffee, original and unique products, historic tours, horse-drawn carriage rides, and scenic tours by plane.

Please call us today for your escape to the coast!

MONTEREY & VICINITY

BIDE-A-WEE
Motel &
Cottages

221 Asilomar Blvd.
Pacific Grove, CA 93950
(408) 372-2330
Owner: Don Kim
Managers: Sue Keppeler

Accommodations: 9 cottages (1 and 2 bedroom) and 11 rooms (double, queen, and king beds).

Amenities: Color cable TV in each unit, full kitchens, ocean views, and fresh in-room coffee.

Rates: $39.00 - $139.00 per night (off season rates available).

Minimum Stay: None.

Restrictions: None.

BIDE-A-WEE Motel & Cottages is a quaint and quiet motor-inn, located in Pacific Grove, on the tip of the Monterey Peninsula. Pacific Grove, frequently called "Butterfly Town, U.S.A.", is the site of an annual migration of Monarch butterflies, which cluster in the pines and eucalyptus found in the town's west side.

Located in a wooded area on Asilomar Blvd., the BIDE-A-WEE is located just a three minute walk from the ocean, the Point Pinos Lighthouse, and the municipal golf course. Enjoy miles of beautiful bicycle paths, or drive down the "Seventeen Mile Drive", bordered with groves of Monterey Cypress and pines that lead to miles of open shoreline with vast ocean views. Just minutes away is the world famous Monterey Bay Aquarium, which offers a spectacular underwater view of the Monterey Bay and it's inhabitants, as well as the popular sea otter habitat, tide pool excursions and hands-on exhibits for children of all ages.

The BIDE-A-WEE is a ten minute drive away from Carmel and all Monterey attractions. Some of the finest restaurants and shops are within a five minute drive.

All of our units are fully furnished and bedding, linen, towels, and coffee are provided. Most cottages have complete kitchens, others have refrigerators, coffee-pots and toasters; all units have individual showers and/or bath.

The cozy atmosphere of the BIDE-A-WEE Motel & Cottages offers you a relaxing and peaceful stay at the Monterey Peninsula.

Merrybrook Lodge

13420 Big Basin Way
P.O. Box 845
Boulder Creek, CA 95006
(831) 338-6813
Owners: Raj & Leela Patel

Accommodations: Cabins and motel units.

Amenities: Kitchens, porches, woodstoves or fireplaces, and electric heat.

Rates: $98.00 - $140.00 per night for 2 persons. Additional person $10.00.

Minimum Stay: Two nights on weekends.

Restrictions: 72 hours cancellation. Holidays require a one week notice.

Merrybrook Lodge is located in the enchanted Valley of the Redwoods surrounded by the green-carpeted and wooded Santa Cruz mountains. An abundance of fern and wildflowers make this an inspiring setting of natural beauty. Rest and relax in this quiet, peaceful wonderland with it's warm days and cool nights.

Individual cottages are attractively furnished in a picturesque grove of redwood trees bordering on the banks of Boulder Creek. Some cottages overlook this sparkling mountain stream with a roomy porch to enjoy this panoramic view. All are large units with living room, bedroom, kitchen and showers to accommodate two to four persons. All come complete with woodstoves or fireplaces, electric heat and completely equipped for your every need.

Spacious motel units are available with morning coffee and small refrigerators. Complete privacy is a plus.

Merrybrook Lodge is located on Big Basin Hwy. three blocks west of State Route #9 which runs through Boulder Creek. Close by are fine restaurants, markets, movies, and fishing and swimming in the San Lorenzo River. Just a short drive away is Big Basin State Park, Cowell Redwoods State Park, the Santa Cruz beach, and the Boulder Creek Golf Course.

Ripplewood Resort

Hwy. 1
Big Sur, CA 93920
(831) 667-2242
Owners: Ray & Celia Sanborn

Accommodations: 16 cabins.

Amenities: Fireplaces, river cabins, and linens.

Rates: $45.00 - $75.00 per night.

Minimum Stay: Two nights on weekends.

Restrictions: No pets. No personal checks. 72 hours cancellation policy.

Ripplewood Resort is located in the heart of the Big Sur Valley. We have 16 cabins, cafe, grocery store, and a Chevron gas station. Our cafe serves breakfast and lunch with homemade sticky buns. Cabin 1: Large cabin with a living room, kitchen, separate bedroom (queen and double bed), deck, and stone fireplace.

Cabin 2: In a secluded area alongside the river. This cabin features a large deck, kitchen, and queen bed.

Cabin 3: Cabin on the river with a deck, queen bed, and kitchen.

Cabin 4: Fireplace cabin along the river with a deck, queen bed, and kitchen.

Cabin 5: Fireplace cabin in the redwoods near the river with a queen bed, and kitchen.

Cabin 6: Cabin with a picture view of the river with a queen bed, and kitchen.

Cabin 7: Fireplace cabin with a separate bedroom, queen bed, and kitchen.

Cabin 8: Fireplace cabin with a deck, separate bedroom, double and queen beds, and a kitchen.

Cabin 9: Cabin, deck over the river with a queen bed, and kitchen.

Cabin 10: Large cabin with fireplace, queen, 2 single beds.

Cabin 11: Motel room type cabin, queen, and double bed.

Cabin 12A and 12B: Duplex cabin with a double bed in each unit.

Cabin 14: Stone fireplace, separate bedroom, queen bed, and kitchen.

Cabin 15: Largest cabin with stone fireplace, queen, double, and single bed, kitchen, and bathroom with a shower/tub. Living room has hand-hewed redwood beams in the ceiling. One other cabin is available. Call for details.

Robles del Rio Lodge

200 Punta del Monte
Carmel Valley, CA 93924
(831) 659-3705
(800) 833-0843
(831) 659-5157 FAX
Owners: Gurries Family

Accommodations: 33 rooms, suites, and cottages.

Amenities: Heated pool, jacuzzi spa, sauna, tennis court, trail rides, on-site restaurant and cantina bar.

Rates: $89.00 - $189.00 per night.

Minimum Stay: One night (during the week). Two nights (on weekends).

Restrictions: No pets.

Set on a ridge top, high above the village of Carmel Valley, 13 miles (and beyond the fog) inland from Carmel and Monterey, Robles del Rio Lodge opened for business in 1928. The rustic hillside resort is a popular site for weddings, and many couples return year after year for anniversary celebrations. Vacationers, honeymooners, corporate groups, titans of industry, and Hollywood stars continue to seek out the Robles del Rio Lodge for the chance to unwind and to savor the tranquility of a by-gone era -- Arthur Murray, Red Skelton, Alistair Cooke, Doris Day, Merv Griffin, Joan Fontaine, Kim Novak, Tippi Hedron, James Woods, the stars of the soap *Santa Barbara*, and 49er coach Bill Walsh are but a few of the many luminaries who have visited and stayed at the lodge over the years. People, whose parents first brought them here as little kids decades ago, frequently return with their own children and grandchildren. Robles Del Rio is one of those rare places that thrives because dedicated guests return time and again and spread the word to their friends and associates.

Knotty Pine and Oak Leaf rooms offer twin and queen beds, private baths, and tranquil views.

Lodge Suites are ideal for honeymooners and anniversary celebrators. These two room suites are interconnected by French doors and offer awesome views.

The Laurel, Bay, Toyon, Oak, and Oak Meadow Cottages feature original 1928 board and batten paneling. They have fireplaces and private bedrooms (Oak Meadow - two bedroom) with queen beds, kitchenettes and full kitchens, and queen sofa sleeper in the living room.

The Fireside Room in the main lodge is a common area where continental breakfast is served every morning from 8 -10 a.m. Groups may use this room for meetings and guests relax by the fire. The on-site Ridge Restaurant offers breathtaking views and award-winning California/French cuisine.

Villa Vista

2-2800 E. Cliff Dr.
Santa Cruz, CA
(831) 866-2626
villavis@1x.netcom.com
www.villavista.com
Owners: Ginger & Bob Good

Accommodations: 2-three bedroom/bath units.

Amenities: Departure cleaning, view of Pacific Ocean, surfers, sunsets, and city lights.

Rates: $1500.00 - $2600.00 per week.

Minimum Stay: Three nights ($900.00).

Restrictions: No pets. No smoking.

Villa Vista combines a timeless beachfront view with the most modern appliances and furnishings to create a warm, comfortable setting for your vacation/retreat.

Each of two units has:

- a spacious living room
- three master bedrooms/baths to accommodate six comfortably

127

- a fully equipped gourmet kitchen with microwave and Cuisinart
- an outdoor view area with patio furniture, spa, and BBQ
- entertainment center including books, board games, and telephone
- washer/dryer, linens

Villa Vista is a year round vacation retreat for couples, a conference, or a family. There are activities nearby including the Boardwalk, Monterey/Carmel, and world-class golf courses. Superb local restaurants tempt too.

But what guests love most is simply the view and the ambiance that Villa Vista provides. They come to relax and rejuvenate, and then they remember and return!

Visitors at Villa Vista have shared the following with us:

"Great time, beautiful place. Fun enjoyed by all."

"...and in the end we got what we hoped for – peace, beauty, and a treasure chest of memories."

CENTRAL SIERRA

Apple Tree Inn

1110 Hwy. 41
P.O. Box 41
Fish Camp, CA 93623
(559) 683-5111
Owners: Vivien & Gerry Smith

Accommodations: 6 cottages.

Amenities: Fireplaces, TV's, porches, and breakfast brought to your cottage.

Rates: $85.00 - $100.00 per night.

Minimum Stay: Two nights on weekends and holidays.

Restrictions: No pets. Three cottages are non-smoking.

Apple Tree Inn offers tranquility and privacy in its spacious, but cozy cottages. The cottages, some with fireplaces, are set on a forested hillside of seven acres dotted with fir trees and wildflowers at 5,000 feet.

Nature's best awaits you during your stay at Apple Tree Inn in a cottage for two persons such as "Little Red" or "Long View" with a fireplace and kingsize bed or "Skyview" and "Birchwood" without fireplaces. "Alpine Haus" has a fireplace and kitchen. "The Little Cottage" can accommodate four persons with a fireplace and kitchen. Homemade muffins and bread, along with fruit, juice and beverage are brought to the cottages each morning so that guests may enjoy breakfast in bed or on the porch.

Yosemite National Park, with its internationally known waterfalls and sculptured granite cliffs, are just two miles away. Giant sequoias can be found at the Mariposa Grove and Nelder Grove. History lives at Wawona, just six miles inside Yosemite National Park with the Yosemite Pioneer History Center. You'll also find the oldest mountain golf course in California at Wawona.

Sit on your porch and listen to the lonesome steam whistle or take a ride on the Yosemite Mountain Sugar Pine Railroad through the Sierra National Forest over old tracks once used for logging trains at the turn of the century. For a taste of the great outdoors take a guided trail ride on a horse with Yosemite Trails Pack Station or a wagon ride.

Take a leisurely walk along Apple Tree Inn's paths through the woods or hike on miles of old logging roads with sweeping views of Mt. Raymond, Big Creek, and Lewis Creek Valleys.

You will find four seasons at the Apple Tree Inn each with its own special appeal. Autumn colors and Indian summer weather highlight the fall, while winter snow provide magically beautiful scenery and snow fun of all types.

Experience the beauty of the Sierras, the splendor of Yosemite, and the quiet charm of Fish Camp by staying at the Apple Tree Inn where moments become memories.

Bass Lake Vacation Rentals

P.O. Box 507
Bass Lake, CA 93604
(559) 642-2211
Owners: Yosemite West Lodging, Inc.

Accommodations: Smaller private cottages and cabins, fully equipped.

Amenities: Complete kitchens, fireplaces, color cable TV with VCR, free local telephone service, BBQ, and decks/patios.

Rates: $135.00 - $195.00 per night; $635.00 - $975.00 (six to seven night stays). Off season rates are lower.

Minimum Stay: Two nights.   Three nights during holidays. One night during off-season.

Restrictions: No pets.   Only registered guests allowed on the premises.

Bass Lake Vacation Rentals cater to singles, couples, and small families, providing cottages and cabins with one or two bedrooms, living room, full-size kitchens, and private baths. Most offer privacy and seclusion, allowing guests to more fully enjoy their deck/patio and yard.   This makes Bass Lake Vacation

Rentals perfect for that romantic getaway or for families wishing to savor the mountain beauty of Bass Lake.

One of our most popular units is the Honeymoon Cottage. This one bedroom cottage has a stone fireplace in the living room, king bed in the bedroom, bath with shower-tub combination, and full-size kitchen (with dishwasher, microwave, and electric-drip coffeemaker). It also features both a large patio with barbecue and a large deck with plenty of room to stretch out, soak up some sun, or relax in the shade while enjoying the view of the lake and mountains in the distance. The Honeymoon Cottage rents for $135/night plus tax; ask about off-season special rates (October through March, non-holiday). The Honeymoon Cottage is available year round.

Bass Lake features an 1800 acre lake nestled among tall mountains, providing fishing, swimming, boating, water skiing, and jet skiing on the lake. Hiking, picnicking, and trips to the surrounding high country are also popular. Day trips to Yosemite National Park, various areas of Sierra National Forest, and to local attractions round out your options. In nearby Oakhurst, you'll find ample shopping for antiques and arts, bowling, and a five-screen cinema, as well as classic melodrama theater on summer weekends.

Bass Lake is easy to reach. Just an hour north of Fresno off Hwy. 41, it's about a four hour drive from the San Francisco Bay Area, four hours from San Luis Obispo, and five hours from Los Angeles. Bass Lake is in a mountain setting with green forests of tall pines and cedars adjoining sandy beaches. Goat Mountain dominates the skyline at one end of the lake; a popular day hike is to the top of Goat Mountain, with it's fantastic view of Bass Lake and the high country.

Big Pine Resort Cottages

P.O. Box 879
Big Pine, CA 93513-0879
(960) 938-2922
Owners: Richard & Joann Lutito

Accommodations: 4 cottages all with full kitchens.

Amenities: Color T.V.'s, fully equipped kitchens, including coffee, pots, toaster, can opener, cooking & eating utensils, fish cleaning area, and BBQ's.

Rates: $40.00 per night (summer), $35.00 per night (winter).

Minimum Stay: One night except certain holidays.

Restrictions: Pets not to be left alone in cottages. Reservations must be made at least 10 days in advance. Deposit required.

Big Pine Resort Cottages is located in the heart of the beautiful Owens Valley on U.S. Hwy. 395 in the town of Big Pine. Big Pine is just a 4 1/2 hour drive north from the Los Angeles area, and about 4 hours south of the Reno, Lake Tahoe area. Here in Big Pine we have three restaurants, two country markets, two fuel and automotive service stations, and tackle shops.

The cottages feature separate living rooms, bedrooms with queen beds and a completely furnished kitchen with freshly brewed coffee. There are four cottages that will sleep four people. A roll-away bed is also available. Pets are welcome with some restrictions.

From our locations, travelers can visit the ancient Bristlecone Forest, just 23 miles from Big Pine. The Bristlecone Pines are the oldest known living things in the world. They are more than 1500 years older than the oldest Redwoods. Some are 4700 years old.

For great trout fishing, we have the Owens River plus many streams and creeks only a few minutes away. Some other very interesting and fun things to do include visiting the Law's Railroad Museum, the Fish Springs Hatchery, Klondike Lake for water skiing, sailing, windsurfing and swimming, and mountain hiking. There is a great opportunity for photography at the beautiful Palisade Glacier, the southern most glacier in the U.S. as well as the Tule Elk Herd and the Sierra Nevada and White Mountain Ranges. For directions to any of these places check with the Big Pine Chamber of Commerce or call (760) 938-2114.

For the ski enthusiasts that visit us in the winter months, we are just one hour away from the Mammoth Mountain slopes and we offer room rates for about 1/2 to 2/3 less than you would have to pay there. Come and visit us and enjoy the fresh clean air, star-filled sky, peaceful atmosphere and friendly people of Big Pine. Mention reading about us in this book at the time of making your reservations and receive a 10% discount.

Caples Lake Resort

P.O. Box 88
Kirkwood, CA 95646
(209) 258-8888
(209) 258-8888 FAX
Owner: John M. Voss

Accommodations: 7 housekeeping cabins and 8 guest rooms in lodge.

Amenities: Cabins come with kitchens, bathrooms and linens. General store, marina boat rental/launch, mountain bike rentals, and sauna.

Rates: Cabins ($65.0 - $140.00); guest rooms ($30.00 - $60.00).

Minimum Stay: Two nights on weekends. Five nights in cabins (July-August).

Restrictions: No pets. No smoking.

Welcome to Caples Lake Resort, nestled in the majestic Sierra Nevada with surrounding mountains reaching 10,000 feet. Located on Caples lake, the resort is open year round for the outdoor enthusiast, fisherman, hiker, photographer and skier, who prefers the unspoiled beauty and rustic, friendly atmosphere of a quiet mountain resort.

Lodging at Caples Lake consists of seven housekeeping cabins, each equipped with full kitchens and bathrooms, all with cookware, utensils and bath and bed linens. The eight guest rooms in the lodge look out over Caples Lake and have separate mens' and womens' bathroom facilities across the hall.

Hiking the unspoiled natural beauty of the High Sierra offers the most experienced outdoor enthusiast a thrill beyond compare. You will delight in the search for wildflowers and wildlife, panoramic vistas of the Carson Pass area, towering peaks, alpine meadows, and the historic path of the Emigrant Trail.

Trout fishing in Caples Lake is well known for its quality and variety of trout species. Numerous small lakes and snow fed streams provide fantastic fly fishing opportunities. Guide services for both are available.

The resort has a general store to provide for all of your camping and fishing needs. The marina has a concrete launch ramp, motor boat rentals, kayaks, canoes, paddle boats, and trails. There is also a Finnish sauna for guest enjoyment. There are seven golf courses located within an hours drive of the resort. Other activities include horseback riding, dog sled rides, snowmobiling, and a trip to the local hot springs.

The resort is located off Hwy. 88, 60 miles west of Jackson and 30 miles south of Lake Tahoe. The main lodge looks out over Caples Lake and has a cozy lounge and fantastic gourmet restaurant to compliment the rustic atmosphere. What a perfect way to end a fantastic day of hiking, fishing, or skiing.

Cedar Crest Resort

P.O. Box 163
Lakeshore, CA 93634
(559) 893-3233 (summer)
(935) 422-8616 (winter)
Owner: Mrs. Dottie Dowdle

Accommodations: 16 cabins, 7 R.V. sites, and 11 tent cottages.

Amenities: Porches, showers, linens, and propane heating. Some cabins have fireplaces and/or kitchens. Restaurant, boat and motor rental, and grocery store.

Rates: $12.00 - $109.00 per night.

Minimum Stay: Two nights. Three nights on holidays.

Restrictions: Deposit refundable only if cancelled 4 weeks prior to date of arrival.

Join us! Escape the heat of the valley and experience the cool, natural beauty of the higher elevations. Cedar Crest Resort is a self-contained summer village located at the mid-point of beautiful Huntington Lake, 68 miles northeast of Fresno. It is at an elevation of 7,000 feet in the Sierra National Forest. Access to the Huntington Lake area is via Hwy. 168 (out of Clovis, CA), a well maintained state highway. Driving time from the San Francisco or Los Angeles area is about five hours.

The Huntington Lake area is famous for sailing, fishing (trout and Kokanee salmon), hiking and as a gateway to the John Muir and Kaiser Wilderness areas. The lake is seven miles long and about one mile wide. Numerous mountain streams feed the lake to test your angling skill or to provide the backdrop for an enjoyable hike.

We have a wide range of clean, comfortable sleeping accommodations to meet everyone's needs. A variety of housekeeping cabins include fully furnished two bedroom bungalows with kitchen and bathroom with shower, floor-to-ceiling glass in the living room and a large porch area overlooking the lake. Cabana units feature a living room/bedroom combination with freestanding fireplace and floor-to-ceiling glass doors, opening onto a large porch, just a stone's throw from the lake.

For those who want something not as primitive as the campgrounds, but more close to nature than the cabins, we offer concrete-floored tent cottages furnished with double cots, woodstoves for cooking, and a picnic table. Restrooms and showers are located in a main facility close to your tent site. For those of you who have a "home on wheels", we provide R.V. sites complete with water and electrical hook-ups and access to the restroom and shower facility.

The Huntington Lake area is unspoiled by development - an emerald gem in a setting of unforgettable beauty. Come and discover Cedar Crest Resort, your family's headquarters for the ideal summer vacation.

Dardanelle Resort

Hwy. 108
Dardanelle, CA 95314
(209) 965-4355
(209) 965-4355 FAX
Owners: Clifford & Joanne Cheney

Accommodations: 4 motel rooms; 8 housekeeping cabins for 2-4 persons; and R.V. park with or without hook-ups.

Amenities: Restaurant, country store, lounge, outside BBQ, and children's play area.

Rates: $55.00 - $99.00 per night (winter rates higher). R.V. rates daily or monthly on request.

Minimum Stay: Three nights on holidays.

Restrictions: No smoking. No pets allowed. In the winter, the road is closed and is accessible by snowmobile only.

The historic Dardanelle Resort, established in 1923, is located on Hwy. 108 just a few miles from the top of Sonora Pass. The resort is surrounded by the beautiful mountains and trees of the Stanislaus National Forest. The middle fork of the Stanislaus River runs along the highway and is easily accessible right across from the resort.

The resort offers a restaurant open for breakfast, lunch and dinner. There are housekeeping cabins with fully equipped kitchens and a four unit motel building equipped with private bathrooms and outside portable barbecues.

A rustic forest setting provides a place for your R.V. with or without hook-ups. Camping spaces are also provided if you prefer tent camping. Bathrooms, showers, and laundry facilities are also available. Gasoline and propane are available and the country store will provide you with fishing licenses, food, snacks, sporting goods, fishing supplies, beer, wine, and souvenirs.

In the summer, hike on the beautiful high Sierra Mountain trails, visit the remote mountain lakes, and take time to enjoy the wildflowers and beautiful scenery. Fish in the river and creeks. Sit around the campfire at night under the starry skies and relax your mind and body.

If you have been dreaming and thinking snow, then the Dardanelle Resort is your place to be for a white winter fun adventure. After your snowmobile journey to the resort, settle in one of our cozy warm cabins, enjoy a warm drink and hot meal at the restaurant, and sit back and relax. When you are ready, prepare to conquer and explore the beautiful snow covered Sonora Pass on your snowmobile. Or pull your snow boots on and explore the surrounding areas such as the Stanislaus River and the ice covered Eagle Creek. For the kid in all of us, build a snowman or challenge your family or friends to a snowball throwing fun time. Take a sled up the mountain side behind the cabins and pretend you are the next Olympic bobsled team. The sky is the limit at Dardanelle Resort!

Darlene's Vacation Cabins

P.O. Box 35
Long Barn, CA 95335
(209) 586-0808, (800) 273-0740, (209) 586-0808 FAX
www.darlenesvacationcabins.com
Owners: Darlene & Eric Jacobson

Accommodations: 18 cabins (from 2 bedrooms/one bath to 6 bedrooms/2 bath).

Amenities: Deck, BBQ, TV/VCR, fireplaces, wood, full kitchens, microwaves, coffee makers, some have dishwashers and washer and dryers.

Rates: $100.00 - $200.00 per night; $575.00 - $850.00 weekly.

Minimum Stay: Two nights. Weekly discount.

Restrictions: No pets. No smoking. Deposits required. No cancellations (we will reschedule).

Our cabins are located in the beautiful areas of Pinecrest, Miwuk, Long Barn, and Cold Springs. These are fully equipped cabin homes. They range in size from two bedrooms with one bathroom to six bedrooms with two bathrooms and can sleep anywhere from 6-15 people comfortably. Each cabin is within close proximity to all of the recreational activities in the Sierra and Motherlode areas.

Fishing, swimming, boating, skiing, hiking, horseback riding, river rafting, gold panning, golfing, tennis, dining, and the theater are many of the activities.

We are open year round. The third night is free if scheduled on a weekend. Please call us for a free brochure. We are located off Hwy. 108, above Twain Harte, at an elevation of 5,000 feet.

Cabin #1: 2 bedroom, 2 bath, sleeps 10, full kitchen, TV/VCR, fireplace and wood, wash/dry, deck, and BBQ.

Cabin #3: 2 bedroom, 1 bath with loft, sleeps 6-8, TV, full kitchen w/microwave and coffee maker, fireplace and wood, washer and dryer, and deck.

Cabin #6: 3 bedroom, 2 bath, sleeps 12, loft, coffee maker, TV, VCR, deck and fireplace, BBQ, wash/dry, and 2 car garage.

Cabin #7: 3 bedroom, 1 1/2 bath, sleeps 10, full kitchen with TV/VCR, fireplace and wood, deck, and BBQ.

Cabin #8: 6 bedroom, 2 bath, sleeps 20, full kitchen with fireplace and wood, TV/VCR, deck, and BBQ.

Cabin #9: 4 bedroom, 2 bath, sleeps 10, full kitchen with dishwasher, fireplace, woodstove with wood, washer and dryer, cable TV, VCR, deck, BBQ, and carport.

Call us for descriptions of cabins 10, 12, 14, 15, 16 and 18.

Dinkey Creek Inn

53861 Dinkey Creek Road
Shaver Lake, CA 93664
(209) 841-3435
Owners: Dennis & Kimberly Beard

Accommodations: 10 chalets.

Amenities: Living room with glass walls, woodburning stoves, satellite TVs, fully equipped kitchens, volleyball, ping pong table and horseshoe pits, private decks with picnic tables, BBQ's, and campfire ring.

Rates: Summer: $85.00-$100.00 per night; $525.00 per week. Winter: $75.00 per night. Ask about our midweek winter specials.

Minimum Stay: Two nights in summer. No minimum in winter.

Restrictions: None

Located in the Sierra National Forest east of Fresno, the Dinkey Creek Inn offers the opportunity to enjoy and explore the majestic, scenic beauty of nature all year long without leaving the comforts of home behind. These new chalets sleep six and offer a private bedroom with a queen bed, kitchen, bath, a living room, and open loft. The kitchen comes fully equipped with dishes, range, and refrigerator. The living room offers a glass wall with views of the surrounding scenery as well as access to a private deck with a picnic table, BBQ, and outdoor campfire ring. The open loft features a queen and two twin beds.

Each chalet is within 200 yards of the scenic wooden trestle bridge. Designated a historical landmark, this is the only free span, redwood timber bridge in the state of California. While standing on the bridge and reading about its history, you can look up or down Dinkey Creek and enjoy it's profusion of wild azaleas, ferns, and "rock-hopping, having-fun" visitors.

Our spring, summer, and fall seasons offer any activity imaginable for all outdoor enthusiasts. There is hiking, biking, swimming, floating on a raft, fishing, horseback riding, nightly outdoor volleyball games, or enjoy movies in the outdoor amphitheater. We also have many fourwheel drive trails in a variety of difficulty ratings.

You can purchase groceries, fishing and camping supplies, hardware, gas, and souvenirs at the store or eat at our cafe. We're famous for our old-fashioned milkshakes.

If you like to enjoy the quiet serenity of snow covered peaks and terrain, you can put on your cross-country skis or snowmobile equipment, and take off on the groomed trails which leave from the chalets to explore our winter wonderland.

Truly family-oriented, and a haven for outdoor activities for any age, we look forward to seeing you at the Dinkey Creek Inn.

Ducey's on the Lake

P.O. Box 109
Bass Lake, CA 93604
(800) 350-7463
(209) 642-3902 FAX
Manager: Maggie Singleton

Accommodations: 20 luxury suites - 10 suites with in-room spa tubs and 2 honeymoon suites with 700 sq. feet of living space, and in-room spa tubs.

Amenities: Fireplaces in all suites, wet bars, refrigerators, continental breakfast delivered to room, tennis, swimming pool, sauna, and jacuzzi.

Rates: $100.00 - $280.00 per night.

Minimum Stay: Two nights (weekends).

Restrictions: No pets.

A perfectly blended design of mountain elegance is what sets Ducey's On The Lake apart.

Twenty lakefront suites with split-level living space are richly appointed as well as spacious. These king units feature a fireplace, wet bar with refrigerator, microwave, remote control television with VCR, and a private lakeside deck. Some rooms also offer in-room spa tubs.

Two honeymoon suites offer a large living room with fireplace and television, wet bar, guest bath, bedroom with fireplace and television, oversized spa tub and shower, and private lakeside deck.

All suites are connected to the dining room and Bar and Grill by private hallways. Swimming pool, jacuzzi, fitness room, gazebo, and lawn area are located adjacent to the lodge overlooking the lake.

For an exceptional dining experience, Ducey's Restaurant promises a superb dinner while enjoying a magnificent view from the water's edge. Menu selections include homemade soups and fresh salads, appetizers, specially prepared beef, chicken, and seafood entrees, and daily prepared desserts. Ducey's is also open for Sunday Brunch.

Ducey's Bar and Grill, located on the upper level, serves appetizers and light meals in season along with complete cocktail service.

Evergreen Lodge

33160 Evergreen Road
Groveland, CA 95321
(209) 379-2606, (800) 935-6343
www.evergreenlodge.com
Owners: John & Kay Bargmann

Accommodations: 18 units, all with shower/bath.

Amenities: Nearby swimming, fishing, tennis, horseback riding, and hiking. BBQ/picnic area. Classic, historic main lodge with restaurant, bar, and general store.

Rates: $70.00 - $100.00 per night.

Minimum Stay: Two nights (weekends).

Restrictions: No pets. Smoking outdoors or in bar only.

Historic Evergreen Lodge was founded in 1921 during the building of Hetch Hetchy reservoir in the northwestern region of Yosemite. Originally, it was a watering hole and meeting place for the thousands of railroad workers and construction workers in the area.

Nestled among the pines, cedars, and oaks in the Stanislaus National Forest, the lodge is within one mile of the Yosemite

Park boundary at an elevation of 4600 feet. The season typically runs from April to October.

Throughout the season, enjoy the wonders of Half Dome, El Capitan, and Yosemite Falls. Venture up to the high country for backpacking or sightseeing along the Tioga Pass and Tuolumne Meadows. Hike to Wapama Falls or Tuealala Falls located across Hetch Hetchy Reservoir. Our friendly staff will introduce you to hidden swimming holes, scenic panoramic views, and local hiking trails.

During summer months, our guests are welcome to enjoy the facilities of San Francisco Camp Mather, a recreation camp located within walking distance of the lodge. Camp Mather offers tennis, horseback riding, a heated swimming pool, a swimming lake, and organized recreational events.

For your convenience, our general store has a complete selection of fishing gear and licenses, backpacking supplies, beer, ice and other groceries and supplies. We also rent bear-proof containers for backpacking into the Yosemite high country.

When the day is done, you'll find great home-cooked meals at reasonable prices in the lodge restaurant, and ice cold beer, cocktails, and frequent entertainment throughout the season in our rustic cocktail lounge.

Or just relax on your rocking chair on the porch of your quiet and comfortable cabin in the forest. All cabins are completely furnished with shower/bath and daily maid service. Evergreen Lodge...the way Yosemite used to be.

Fern Creek Lodge

Rt. 3, Box 7
June Lake, CA 93529
(619) 648-7722
(619) 648-7477 FAX
Owners: Robin and James Hart

Accommodations: 10 cabins, 4 apartment units, all with full kitchens, linens, and TV.

Amenities: Fireplaces in two and four bedroom cabins. Small grocery store on the premises. Covered patio with BBQ's, fireplace and picnic tables. Horseshoe pit. Adjacent to Forest Service property. Beautiful vistas in any direction.

Rates: $47.50 - $200.00 per night.

Minimum Stay: One night.

Restrictions: Pets allowed under special circumstances.

Fern Creek Lodge is located on the beautiful June Lake Loop in the Eastern High Sierra. The Loop has four pristine mountain lakes, as well as streams that are all full of trout. There is plenty of hiking and fishing in the summer, and downhill and cross-country skiing in the winter. Fern Creek Lodge is located close enough to Yosemite for day trips and is within an hour's drive to historic Bodie State Park. Mono Lake, with it's mystery and beauty, is also close by.

Sara, Angel of The Sierras, Meacham's Intended, The Old Schoolhouse, and De Noon are all small rustic cabins with a bedroom, bathroom, and kitchen big enough to eat in. These cabins only sleep two people.

Carson and Gibbs are apartment units with one bedroom, a living room, small kitchen and small eating area, and bathroom. They are in the top of a two-story building. These two units will sleep 4 to 5 people.

Dana and Wood are family units with a small living area/bedroom, separate kitchen, and separate bathroom. They are in the bottom of a two-story building. These two units will sleep up to 6 to 7 people.

Audubon, Lee Wulff, John Muir, and Ansel Adams are two bedroom cabins with one bathroom, living room with fireplace, and a kitchen big enough to eat in. These cabins have a nice sundeck that spans the front of the cabin. They will sleep up to 6 people.

Hearttree and Dutch Lady are four bedroom cabins with two baths, kitchen, large eating area and large living area with a fireplace. They also have a nice sundeck across the front of the cabin. These cabins will sleep up to 14 people.

The grounds at Fern Creek Lodge have lots of trees and grass. It is a beautiful place no matter what time of year you choose to come. There are many restaurants within walking distance or short drive.

The Forks Resort

39150 Road 222
Bass Lake, CA 93604
(559) 642-3737
Owners: Ron & Leslie Cox

Accommodations: 1 and 2 bedroom cabins.

Amenities: Restaurant, general store, marina, and BBQ's.

Rates: $70.00 - $115.00 (per night) or $400.00 - $725.00 (per week).

Minimum Stay: Four nights.

Restrictions: None

The Forks Resort, located on Bass Lake, in the Sierra National Forest, is only fourteen miles from the southern entrance to Yosemite National Park and eight miles from the southern end of the Golden Chain Highway through California's Gold Country. The Forks Resort has built a reputation as a traditional family vacation spot. Family owned and operated for three generations, The Forks Resort has provided quality and consistency year after year to their customers.

The Forks Restaurant, home of the famous "Forks Burger", offers the finest in family dining. Breakfast, lunch, and dinner featuring homemade soups, chili and dressings, are served in the original "50's diner" setting.

The modern cabins, accomodating four to six persons, are located near the lake, most with lake views. One and two bedroom units with kitchens and baths are available. The kitchens are fully equipped with dishes and cooking utensils for your convenience. Fishing, boating, waterskiing, and swimming in Bass Lake are just outside your cabin door. There are numerous hiking trails and three golf courses nearby.

The general store is well stocked with familiar brands of groceries, fresh meats, vegetables and fruits, drug sundries, souvenirs, sporting goods, fishing tackle, propane, gasoline, ice, and boat rentals.

Gables Cedar Creek Inn

22560 Twain Harte Dr.
P.O. Box 1818
Twain Harte, CA 95383
(209) 586-3008, (888) 900-4224
e-mail: info@gocedarcreek.com
www.gocedarcreek.com
Owners: Tim & Jan Ewing

Accommodations: We offer cozy, individually decorated getaways that range from romantic suites and cabins with gas or wood burning fireplaces to two larger homes.

Amenities: All units include bath and/or shower and fully or mini-equipped kitchens. All linens supplied. Color cable TV/VCR, and telephone. Maid service available on request only. Non-smoking units.

Rates: $70.00 - $125.00 per night, double occupancy. $8.00 per night for each additional person in our cabins or cottages. $15.00 for each additional person in our houses.

Minimum Stay: Two nights on weekends. Three or four nights on holidays. Four night minimum in July and August if reservations are made more than one month in advance.

Restrictions: No pets without prior approval.

The Gables Cedar Creek Inn is located in the resort village of Twain Harte, California, just off Hwy 108. Situated in the peace and serenity of tall pine and cedar trees, it is the perfect place to fall in love all over again.

A creek runs through our property but additional rivers, streams and lakes are all close by. Year round recreation activities located nearby include golf, swimming, hiking, fishing, hunting, skiing (water and snow), cave exploring, gold panning, live theater, and much more. There are many fine restaurants for your dining pleasure.

The quiet beauty away from the hustle and bustle of the city awaits you at the Gables Cedar Creek Inn.

The Homestead

41110 Road 600
Ahwahnee, CA 93601
(559) 683-0495
Owners: Cindy Brooks & Larry Ends

Accommodations: 4 newly constructed cottages nestled in the oaks on 160 acres. Each cottage features a living room with fireplace, kitchen and dining area, separate bedroom with queen size bed and large private bathroom. The Star Gazing Loft is smaller and does not have a fireplace.

Amenities: Kitchens are fully equipped with new dishes, cooking pans & utensils, toasters, coffee makers, coffee, tea, juice, fruit, and muffins. Daily maid service, large outdoor barbecue and picnic area, private setting area for each cottage, and Native American historical site. Horse layover available on the property.

Rates: $135.00 - $235.00 per night.

Minimum Stay: Two nights on weekends.

Restrictions: No smoking. Limited accommodations for children at an additional charge. No pets.

The Homestead is a very private and romantic all cottage bed and breakfast on 160 wooded acres. The adobe and stone cottages nestle respectfully among the ancient oaks. Comfortable living rooms with gas fireplaces, romantic bedrooms, spacious bathrooms and inviting country kitchens make each cottage a haven of relaxation and privacy. The warmth of yellow pine and saltillo tile floors grace each cottage with a simple luxury. The Star Gazing Loft has a combined living room, kitchenette and bedroom with a private bathroom.

While the setting is rural, The Homestead provides the modern amenities of satellite television, air conditioning, gas barbecue, maid service, and in cottage massages. Three area golf courses challenge players of all levels. The mountain village of Oakhurst, a ten minute drive, is host to quaint shops, supermarkets and a variety of dining alternatives.

The Homestead can lull you into the slower pace of a mountain retreat where you can relax and do nothing, or serve as your home base for days of adventure in Yosemite and the magnificent Sierra. Proprietors Cindy and Larry are always available to assist you in planning your stay. We invite you to join us and experience a hideaway that flows in tune with nature's quiet rhythm.

The Homestead is located in the town of Ahwahnee, just 2 and ½ miles off Hwy 49. We're below the snowline for easy year-round access.

Kay's Silver Lake Resort

Silver Lake on Hwy 88
48400 Kay's Road
Pioneer, CA 95666
(209) 258-8598
Owner: Mona White

Accommodations: 9 housekeeping cabins.

Amenities: Kitchens with utensils, linens, blankets, and towels.

Rates: $65.00 - $150.00 per night.

Minimum Stay: Two nights.

Restrictions: No pets. No maid service.

Kay's Silver Lake Resort is located on Silver Lake at the 7,300 foot elevation on Hwy. 88, 52 miles east of Jackson and 35 miles southwest of South Lake Tahoe. This portion of Hwy. 88 follows the old "Emigrant Trail" blazed by Kit Carson, and in 1965 received an award for the most scenic highway in the nation.

The resort offers a general store with groceries, dairy products, soda, beer, wine, drugs, hardware, motor oil, and a large selection of fishing tackle. We also have motor boat rentals for fishing, a concrete launch ramp, and overnight beaching for boats. From the first of June through October, most of the trails and back roads are clear of snow, although, there are some snow fields that will last all year long. There are designated trails which accommodate mountain bikes, dirt bikes, four wheel drive, and horses. For just plain old hiking, the Horse Canyon Trail gives you direct access to the Mokelumne wilderness area and 12 miles west is Carson Pass (8565') and the Pacific Crest Trail. Silver Lake has several varieties of trout (Rainbow, German Brown, Brookies, and Mackinaw) for your fishing pleasure as well as boating, horseback riding, and water skiing. For the photographer, the spring flowers bloom in June and July with the fall colors in late September and October. Hunting in the area is generally in October and early November.

November through May we are buried under many feet of snow. Hwy. 88 is very well-maintained in the winter as well as our own parking lot for our cabin guests and store customers. However, there is about a two hundred yard traverse over the snow from the parking lot to our rental cabins. This can be done by hiking with a good pair of snow boots, but it's sometimes easier with cross-country skis or snowshoes.

For winter activities there is ice-fishing, snowmobiling, both Nordic and Alpine skiing, and snowshoeing. The groomed "Silver-Bear" snowmobile trail runs from Silver Lake to Bear River Reservoir (about twenty miles). Kirkwood Meadows is located just five miles from the resort for the best in downhill and cross -country skiing.

Lakeshore Resort

P.O. Box 197
Lakeshore, CA 93634
(559) 893-3193, (559) 893-2193 FAX
e-mail:lakeshore@netptc.net
www.lakeshoreresort.com
Owners: Stephen & Melinda Sherry

Accommodations: 26 rustic mountain cabins and 20 R.V. spaces with full hook-ups.

Amenities: Some cabins with kitchens, mountain saloon with pot-bellied stove, Saturday TV, general store, and restaurant with fireplace.

Rates: $45.00 - $125.00 per night.

Minimum Stay: Two nights (weekends). Three nights (holidays).

Restrictions: Some pets allowed (check with owners). No TVs or telephones in cabins.

Lakeshore Resort, built in 1922 and open year round, is located in the Sierra National Forest at beautiful Huntington Lake off Hwy. 168, an hour and a half from Fresno, at 7,000 feet. Lakeshore consists of 32 pine covered acres, directly across Huntington Lake Road from Huntington Lake and the main boat launch, ramp, and beaches. We're even on the map!

We offer a rustic mountain atmosphere with our completely stocked mountain market with antiques & collectibles, cozy family style restaurant, saloon with large rafters, 2 dart boards, satellite TV, and friendly people. Our 3,000 sq. ft. dance hall hosts private and public parties, dances, sing-alongs, and slide shows. We have 26 cabins which we rent to the public, and a 20 space RV park with full hook-ups, firepits, picnic tables, laundry facilities, and shower rooms.

Huntington Lake has superb sailing in the summer. The wind is consistent, coming up around 10:00 am and lasting until 4:00 pm every day. The weather is warm, skies blue and clear, and the nights cool, with a million stars. Fishing, sailboarding, and swimming are also to be enjoyed. D & F Pack Station is a short walk up the road for trail rides. Boat rental facilities are located at both ends of the lake. The Forest Service offers nature talks and hikes.

In the fall and winter, Lakeshore provides cozy cabins with flannel sheets and heated mattress pads on all of it's queen size beds for skiers, snowmobilers, and snow players. Sierra Summit Ski Area is 2 1/2 miles away. In the spring and fall off season rates are in effect.

Lakeshore is family owned and operated. In 2000, we celebrated 78 years of operation. Come and visit our RUSTIC escape where R stands for restful, rural and rugged; U stands for unique; S stands for simple and sunny; T stands for trees and terrific; I stands for interesting and inviting; and C stands for country, cozy, and casual.

Lazy Z Resort

P.O. Box 1055
Twain Harte, CA 95383
(209) 586-3857 FAX
(800) 585-1238
Owners: The Zelinsky Family

Accommodations: 6 cabins with kitchens, bath, TV, VCR, BBQ, deck, and patio. Sleeps 2 to 6 people.

Amenities: Lodge, pool, jacuzzi, table tennis, horseshoes, walking trails, near golf, fishing, hiking, boating, and shopping.

Rates: $95.00 - $157.00 per night (weekly); $105.00 - $175.00 per night (weekends). Weekly discount rates. Seasonal packages available.

Minimum Stay: Two nights. Flexible during off season.

Restrictions: Two night minimum may apply - please inquire. No pets. Seven day cancellation notice required (fourteen days during holidays and June - September).

The Lazy Z Resort is a hidden oasis nestled among tall pines and fragrant cedars. Located in the heart of the Gold Country at 3,500 ft. elevation, you'll find a peaceful setting only minutes from the town of Twain Harte (off Hwy 108 – Sonora Pass).

163

The resort features a unique swimming pool which looks as though it were carved out of mountain granite with cascading waterfalls. After a swim, relax in the jacuzzi, or lounge by the poolside, where you can take advantage of our tropical outdoor cabana, just waiting to be used to entertain your friends and family for that special gathering. Step over for a game of table tennis or to the horseshoe area where future champions practice! Perhaps a stroll along our mountain walkways may be just in order for you and your family, or just snuggle up to a cozy fire in the Lodge.

Our 6 cabins offer first class accommodations and are open year round. Each cabin is uniquely different, newly remodeled, beautifully decorated and ranges in size to accommodate from 2 to 6 people. You will find a kitchen and bathroom in each cabin with fireplaces in most (firewood supplied) plus TV, VCR, and stereo add to the luxury and comfort. We supply everything in the cabins except food.

Every season has it's own beauty and activities, from snow and water skiing, to golf, tennis, hiking, and fishing. There are plenty of historical sites, restaurants and shops only minutes away. The Lazy Z Resort is a lure to a clientele that includes movie stars, sports figures, and other notables who want a relaxing break from the public spotlight.

The Zelinsky Family welcomes you for a weekend getaway, family fun, weddings, reunions, or retreats. Special rates and packages are available in every season, for every occasion, so please ask! Please call us for a free brochure.

Pinecrest Chalet Resort

P.O. Box 1279
500 Dodge Ridge Rd.
Pinecrest, CA 95364
(209) 965-3276 / (209) 965-3849 FAX
e-mail: pchalet@mlode.com
www.pinecrestchalet.com
Owners: Marvin & Karen Taylor

Accommodations: Cabins, townhouses, and RV park.

Amenities: Swimming pool, sand volleyball, basketball, horseshoes, and playground.

Rates: $65.00 (1 queen bed) to $265.00 (4 bedroom, 2 bath townhouse); $29.50 for RV park. Group/weekly discounts available.

Minimum Stay: Two nights peak periods (winter weekends & summer). Three nights (holiday weekends).

Restrictions: 14-30 day cancellation period depending on size of unit and holiday time period.

Located in California's High Sierra Nevada Mountains and surrounded by the beautiful Stanislaus National Forest, Pinecrest Chalet Resort is a year-round vacation getaway nestled quietly in seven acres of whispering pines. Guests choose from a wide variety of accommodations to meet the vacation lodging needs of any size family or group.

Popular mini-chalets promise quaint lodging in one-room cabin suites complete with kitchens, woodburning fireplaces, cathedral knotty-pine ceilings, and either two queen beds with shower/bath, or a more intimate chalet with king bed and jacuzzi bathtub.

Spacious townhouses and deluxe cabins offer two to four bedrooms, kitchens, large living rooms with woodburning fireplaces, and decks for family and group entertainment.

If simplicity fits the bill, our economy cabins offer modest lodging at modest prices. These one room bungalows sleep two to four and include shower baths.

A small on-site RV Park has full hook-up sites and can accommodate any size recreational vehicle.

Pinecrest Chalet Resort's combination of cabins, townhouses and RV Park allows families and groups the option of enjoying a variety of vacation experiences in one location. Along with the many family-oriented amenities that our resort offers, you can also enjoy a quiet stroll along the North Fork Tuolumne River that flows throughout the seven-acre property.

We are close to fishing, boating, hiking, and horseback riding. Winter activities include downhill and cross-country skiing, ice-skating, sledding and snowboarding (just 3 miles away at Dodge Ridge Winter Sports Area).

Pine Tree Retreat

4118 Guadalupe Cr. Rd.
Mariposa, CA 95338
(209) 966-3106
(209) 966-3106 FAX
e-mail: pianovan@yosemite.net
park.yosemite.net/yosemitepine
Owners: Pam & Bill Vanderveer

Accommodations: 4 bedroom house (sleeps 1-8); 2 bedroom house (sleeps 1-4).

Amenities: Kitchens, TV's, BBQ's, and decks.

Rates: 4 bedroom house ($175.00 per night for 1-8 people); 2 bedroom house ($140.00 per night for 1-4 people); add'l person $10.00; 7th night free. $50.00 refundable security deposit required.

Minimum Stay: Two nights. Three nights on holidays.

Restrictions: No pets. Two week cancellation policy - three weeks on holidays.

The Pine Tree Retreat is surrounded by pine trees in a subdivision of Yosemite National Park called Yosemite West. It is near Chinquapin, at the turnoff to Glacier Point in Yosemite on

Hwy. 41. At an elevation of 5,000 feet, it is only six miles to Badger Pass Ski Resort, twelve miles to Yosemite Valley and Village and twelve miles to Wawona.

The houses are fully furnished. All sheets and towels are provided. The kitchens are fully equipped with microwaves, coffee pots, toasters, full stoves, and refrigerators.

There are endless activities in Yosemite National Park year round. In the winter there is downhill skiing at Badger Pass, sledding and cross-country skiing trails all over the park, including trails within one mile of the Retreat. In the spring, the waterfalls and Merced River are at their fullest, flowing beautifully. Of course, there is hiking and backpacking all year long. In the summer, swimming and horseback riding are very popular. In the fall, gorgeous colors are abundant as the plants and trees get ready for winter.

After a day of exploring Yosemite National Park, one of nature's most spectacular achievements, you can relax in the comforts and modern conveniences of a home.

Powderbears Accommodations

P.O. Box 5002
Bear Valley, CA 95223
(209) 753-2136
(209) 753-2136 FAX
Owner: Phil and Aneta Davis

Accommodations: 2 bedroom log cabin and a 3 bedroom condominium.

Amenities: Fireplace, washer/dryer, deck, ski locker at lifts, and an oversnow transport to log cabin in winter.

Rates: $150.00 - $250.00 per night. Weekly rates are available.

Minimum Stay: Two nights.

Restrictions: No smoking. Pets must be declared.

Powderbears Accommodations is located in the small resort village of Bear Valley, located at 7,000 feet in the heart of the Sierra Nevada Mountains. Bear Valley is midway between Yosemite National Park and Lake Tahoe.

Our accommodations feature a lovely log cabin with two bedrooms (one bath), a wood/gas cookstove, fireplace, and large deck. The Log Cabin is snowbound six months of the year and transportation of your supplies is by Snowcat. Or you may wish to stay in a modern three bedroom, two bath condominium. Our condo also has a fireplace, a small deck, and is conveniently located in "downtown" Bear Valley, close to restaurants, shops and all the facilities Bear Valley has to offer.

Both kinds of accommodations have a washer/dryer, TV, VCR, and microwave oven, complete kitchens, and all cooking utensils and linens.

World class skiing, both Alpine and Nordic await your winter visits to Bear Valley. In summer there is hiking, mountain bike trails, fishing on numerous, crystal clear streams, boating and sea-kayaking on Lake Alpine, and remote, granite island-studded lakes.

Let Powderbears provide a high mountain experience to be long remembered!

The Redwoods In Yosemite

P.O. Box 2085
Wawona Station
Yosemite National Park, CA 95389
(209) 375-6666
(209) 375-6400 FAX
e-mail: info@redwoodsinyosemite.com
www.redwoodsinyosemite.com
Manager: Joyce Koller

Accommodations: 130 private year round vacation home rentals (1-6 bedrooms).

Amenities: Fully furnished homes with fireplaces or woodburning stoves, some very modern, and some rustic. Near waterfalls, hiking, horseback riding, skiing, and golfing in a forest setting.

Rates: $82.00 per night (low season) to $530.00 per night.

Minimum Stay: Two nights. Three nights (summer/holidays).

Restrictions: Some homes are non-smoking, will accept pets, and are handicap accessible.

Yosemite National Park! In the fall, winter, spring, or summer, this is a gloriously beautiful vacation spot anytime of the year.

And within the park boundaries is a secluded group of privately owned mountain homes and cabins called The Redwoods In Yosemite. The homes range from one bedroom cabins to six bedroom homes.

All of our homes are fully furnished, including linens, dishes, kitchen utensils, BBQ's, and firewood. The Redwoods In Yosemite is located 6 miles inside the south entrance of Yosemite Park, in the community of Wawona. Nearby Chilnualna Falls and the south fork of the Merced River are great places to fish, hike, and swim.

Mariposa Grove of the Giant Sequoias is approximately 8 miles from The Redwoods In Yosemite, and the Valley is a 24 mile drive. For skiers, Badger Pass is 17 miles from The Redwoods In Yosemite, and golfers will find the Wawona Golf Course to be a challenge in the spring and summer months.

Our larger homes are well-suited for business "retreats" and "brain-storming" sessions. A combination of smaller homes can accommodate a group, or select the perfect cabin for your family vacation. Two nearby meeting rooms can be rented for your group or family gathering.

The Redwoods In Yosemite is open all year. Two small grocery stores are close by as is a gas station, and seasonal gift shop. The historic Wawona Hotel is within a mile of The Redwoods In Yosemite and offers the visitor breakfast, casual lunch, and fine dining.

Reverse Creek Lodge

Rt. 3, Box 2
June Lake, CA 93529
(760) 648-7535, (800) 762-6440
e-mail: reverse@qnet.com
reversecreeklodge.com
Owners: Ed & Linda Ransford

Accommodations: Cabins and A-Frames.

Amenities: Great views, color TV, skiing, fishing, hiking, hot springs, horseback riding, BBQ's, picnic areas, and lots of sight seeing.

Rates: $55.00 - $100.00 per night. Discount "4-night" special. $8.00 per night for each additional person.

Minimum Stay: One night.

Restrictions: No pets.

Reverse Creek Lodge is located in the picturesque June Lake Loop, quietly nestled in the Eastern Sierra Nevada. June Lake once was used as a hideaway for many Hollywood stars. Today, June Lake offers the perfect getaway all year long. With four beautiful lakes within the 14 mile scenic "Loop" drive, June Lake offers some of the best fishing in the Sierra Nevada plus swimming, sailing, boardsailing, powerboating, and water-skiing.

Go hiking and horseback riding within the grandeur of the Ansel Adams Wilderness area. Or for the adventurer, visit many of the Eastern Sierras attractions like Mono Lake Tufa Reserve and Bodie State Park (one of the best ghost towns in California). Take the Tioga Pass to one of the most beautiful national parks in the country - Yosemite. Or travel to nearby Mammoth Lakes to see the amazing Devil's Postpile.

Just as summer is full of activities, wintertime brings the true majesty to June Lake. Alpine Village comes alive with winter sports and June Mountain Ski Resort offers miles of vertical skiing. For those who like solitude, June Lakes is abundant with groomed trails for cross-country skiing.

The Reverse Creek Lodge offers several different options for lodging. Our cabins range from motel units for 1-2 persons (color TV, kitchenette, shower), to one bedroom units for 1-2 persons (color TV, full kitchen, and shower). For 1-4 persons, we have a large one bedroom or regular two bedroom unit (color TV, full kitchen, and shower) to a large two bedroom unit for 1-6 persons (color TV, full kitchen, and shower). These cabins are off the highway, nestled among the pines next to Reverse Creek.

We have four chalets (A-Frames) which will house anywhere from 1-2 persons to 1-6 persons. Each comes with a color TV, full bath (one has 2 baths), and one has a kitchen. There is a beautiful view from each of these deluxe A-Frame chalets.

Sequoia Village Inn

45971 Sierra Drive
P.O. Box 1014
Three Rivers, CA 93271
(559) 561-3652
(559) 561-3628
Owners: Curt, Laurie & Adam Nutter

Accommodations: 8 housekeeping cottages and chalets with bathrooms (sleeps 2 - 12 people).

Amenities: Pool, hot tub, spa, some fireplaces, BBQ, outdoor fireplaces, hiking trail adjacent to Sequoia/Kings Nat'l Park, herb garden, restaurant across the street, raft trips, fishing, color cable TV/VCRs, and air conditioning. Kitchens come with microwaves, coffeemakers & grinders.

Rates: $61.00 - $218.00 per night.

Minimum Stay: One night. Three nights on holidays.

Restrictions: One week cancellation policy. Holidays must give two weeks notice.

Why not experience the wonder of Sequoia Kings National Park with a relaxing stay at Sequoia Village Inn! A cluster of quaint cottages and chalets at 1,200 feet, Sequoia Village Inn is located overlooking the Marble Fork and East Fork of the Kaweah River.

The entrance station to Sequoia/Kings Canyon National is located one minute up the road from the Inn. The Inn is located about 36 miles east of Visalia on Hwy 198. We are about six miles past the scenic Sierra Foothill town of Three Rivers and directly left after the Gateway Bridge. The fine dinner house, The Gateway, is directly across from us.

The property was once the campground of the Monache Indians as evidenced by the lush oak groves and native vegetation and mortar holes. An aqueduct and trail separates the grounds from the National Park. Enjoy a morning jog or scenic hike along the 3 1/2 mile path.

The comfortable housekeeping cottages are full of country charm and freshly cut flowers. Accommodations range from two story chalets and one story cottages to a roomy duplex unit. The cottages feature complete kitchens with everything from a microwave to freshly ground coffee you grind and then make yourself. Coffee, tea, hot chocolate and popcorn are found in baskets in the kitchens. Two cottages have fireplaces with fires built for you and a supply of wood. Patios surround each cottage and offer guests a chance to greet the sun, gaze at stars in the clear mountain sky, or listen to the river.

Your hosts at Sequoia Village, Curt, Laurie and Adam, are local longterm residents who are very familiar with National Park activities. They can give you ideas for hiking trails, town events and secret spots to visit that will make your trip a memorable one. A swimming pool and hot tub are also available.

Silver City

Mineral King
Recreation Area
P.O. Box 56
Three Rivers, CA 93271
(559) 561-3223 (summer)
(559) 734-4109 (winter), (805) 528-2730
e-mail: silvercity@thegrid.net
www.silvercityresort.com
Owners: Norman & Connie Pillsbury

Accommodations: 10 rustic cabins and 4 deluxe Swiss chalets.

Amenities: Kitchens, outdoor decks, campfire rings, and BBQ's; 3 deluxe chalets with full kitchens, showers, living rooms, and views.

Rates: $70.00 - $250.00 per night.

Minimum Stay: One night in cabins. Two nights in chalets. Seasonal: Open Memorial day to November 1.

Restrictions: No pets. No smoking. No camping on grounds.

Silver City is a rustic family resort nestled among pines and cedars at 7,000 feet in the Sequoia National Park. Privately owned and cared for by the same family for 60 years, Silver City offers the best of the "old days" and the comfort of the new.

Our 10 rustic cabins, built in the 1930's, have the feel of the simple life -- with woodburning stoves, basic kitchens, kerosene and propane lamps, outdoor decks adjacent to a campfire ring and babbling creeks nearby. These rustic cabins each have their own charm and personality from the one-room cozy "sleeping" cabin for two, to the two-bedroom "Highview" cabin for six, with it's own bathroom, kitchen, refrigerator and a spectacular view.

The new deluxe Swiss Chalets are large and spacious, accommodating eight people. The three bedrooms, full bath, beautiful kitchen and breathtaking views make these very popular for family groups. The new in 2000 "mini-chalet" is perfect for 2-4 people.

The Silver City Restaurant and bakery, located adjacent to the cabins, serves delicious, homemade food. The Silver City Mountain Store carries camping and backpacking supplies, fishing tackle, food, souvenirs, and gifts of all kinds.

The main reason that Silver City and the Mineral King area have remained such a wonderful secret is the Mineral King Road which contains 650 curves with incredible scenery all along the way.

We offer you the best hiking in the Sierras, from meadows steeped with wildflowers to the pristine Alpine lakes. Take a hike to the nearby lakes or to the ancient Redwoods, or just relax on your deck and watch the deer graze, chipmunks scurry busily about, and listen to the sound of the birds. We offer you the gift of "quiet". Come and enjoy the best kept secret of the Sierras - Silver City!

The Strawberry Inn

P.O. Box 61
Strawberry, CA 95375
(209) 965-3662
(800) 965-3662
Owners: Brian & Mary Sutherland

Accommodations: 15 rooms at the Inn, and 8 three bedroom – two bathroom cabins that sleep 8.

Amenities: Private in-room baths, fishing, hiking, skiing, snowmobiling, small craft boating, and a beach nearby.

Rates: $75.00 per night (2 queen beds). $6.00 roll away. 10% discount for seniors. Group and weekly discounts available.

Minimum Stay: Two nights on weekends. Three nights in cabins.

Restrictions: No pets. 10 day cancellation policy (holidays - must give 2 weeks notice).

High in the Sierras, nestled among tall pines, the Sutherland Family welcomes you with courteous old-fashioned hospitality and joy! Everything is here to please you from our personal attention, to nature's vast seasonal array of beauty.

The Strawberry Inn, retaining it's true country charm is open all year. Located on Hwy. 108 (the Sonora Pass) in Strawberry, it is an easy drive from the San Francisco Bay Area and valley locations. Here you have the setting for a marvelous balance of outdoor fun, mountain relaxation, and superb dining pleasure that your family will love.

Choose from fly-fishing in the Stanislaus River right in our own backyard, or in nearby Pinecrest Lake, or hike on miles of trails that wind through the majestic Sierra. Family skiing is only minutes away at Dodge Ridge Ski Resort where you can enjoy downhill skiing. Cross-country trails are nearby. Whichever you choose, there are many adventures to be had in this magnificent outdoor setting.

Dining in the restaurant by the river which overlooks a serene setting will kindle warm memories long afterwards. Mouth-watering entrees are a mix of California Cuisine, South-western, and Continental and are sure to please even the youngest members of your family.

You will enjoy relaxing in our newly remodeled (from floor to rafters) rooms and cabins. Quaint and spacious, each is accommodated with a private bath.

Strawberry Inn is the perfect choice for weddings, reunions, birthdays, retreats, and anniversaries. Our Inn's staff will personally help coordinate your special event to create an occasion to cherish.

Yosemite Region Resorts

P.O. Box 19
Groveland, CA 95321
(209) 962-4396
(800) 962-4765
e-mail: realfun@mtnleisure.com
www.mtnleisure.com
Owners: John & Sandra Stone

Accommodations: Cabins, condos, and homes (all fully equipped).

Amenities: 18 hole championship golf course, 4 lighted tennis courts, lake with sailing, swimming, boating, and fishing.

Rates: $77.00 - $225.00 per night.

Minimum Stay: Some units one night minimum. Some units one week minimum.

Restrictions: No pets.

Pine Mountain Lake is located at Groveland, 26 miles west of Yosemite on Hwy. 120 and 126 miles east of San Francisco at an elevation of 3,000 feet.

Lake Tulloch and Lake Don Pedro are approximately 110 miles east of San Francisco, at slightly lower elevations.

Our beautiful areas and resort communities offer many activities for the entire family.

Pine Mountain Lake, with six miles of shoreline, has three sandy beaches where you can enjoy sunning, swimming, fishing, boating, and horseback riding. Renters are now allowed to put their own boats on Pine Mountain Lake, and small boat rentals are available at the Marina.

For serious waterskiers, Lake Tulloch and Lake Don Pedro are exactly what you are looking for. Call us for vacation rentals where your boat has it's own private dock.

Lake Tulloch and Lake Don Pedro also offer beautiful golf courses and similar amenities.

Whatever your desire, our selection of vacation rentals will fit your needs. You may rent a house, condo or cabin on or near the lake, golf course, tennis courts, or in the pines.

Please call for a color brochure and list of rentals including amenities and prices.

Yosemite West Cottages

P.O. Box 36
Yosemite Nat'l Park, CA 95389
(559) 642-2211
Owners: Yosemite West Lodging, Inc.

Accommodations: Studios, apartments, condos, townhouses, duplexes, cabins, cottages, mountain homes, and vacation homes.

Amenities: Fully-equipped kitchens, color TV with VCR, decks, wood-burning fireplaces, bed & bath linens provided.

Rates: $95.00 - $385.00 per night. Off-season rates are lower.

Minimum Stay: Two nights. Three nights (holidays). Four nights (Thanksgiving). Five nights (Christmas/New Year's).

Restrictions: No pets. Only registered guests allowed on premises. No sleeping bags. No motor homes or campers.

Your Yosemite vacation begins with fully-equipped accommodations at Yosemite West, Yosemite's finest lodging area. Tall pines, incense cedars, and silver-tip firs provide a mountain forest setting to greet you each morning and welcome you home each night.

Centrally located to the main areas of Yosemite National Park, you'll find the main areas of the park a short drive away. To the north is the world-famous Yosemite Valley and visitor services in Yosemite Village. Wawona and the majestic Mariposa Grove of Big Trees are to the south. To the east are Washburn Point and Glacier Point, which offer outstanding mountain vistas, and the snow fun of Badger Pass Ski Area, Yosemite's center for downhill and cross-country skiing.

Accommodations provided by Yosemite West Cottages include freshly-made beds (many oversized), one or more baths, completely furnished kitchens or kitchenettes, color TV's with VCR, and outside decks. Most have wood-burning fireplaces (firewood not included). In the winter, your unit is warm upon arrival.

Full-size vacation homes offer a spacious alternative to typical motel rooms. These feature a living room, dining area, full-size kitchen, 1-3 bedrooms and 1-2 baths. Many styles are available including townhomes, duplexes, cabins, cottages, and mountain homes.

Studios and apartment-size units accommodate from 1-4 persons blending sleeping and sitting areas with an apartment-size kitchen and private bath. These are available as duplex and condominium units.

The Yosemite West Cottages reservations staff will assist you in selecting the accommodation to meet all of your needs. Every season at Yosemite offers a new dimension of spectacular natural beauty.

LAKE TAHOE & VICINITY

High Sierra Getaways

P.O. Box 846
Shingle Springs, CA 95682
(530) 677-0410
(530) 677-1424 FAX
e-mail: rich@cedarwestproperties.com
Property Manager: Cedar West Properties

Accommodations: Cabins & vacation homes.

Amenities: Year-round resort area.

Rates: $125.00 - $175.00 per night, excluding holidays.

Minimum Stay: Two nights.

Restrictions: Some units allow pets.

Cedar West Properties offers sales and rentals in the High Sierra between Riverton and South Lake Tahoe, along the Hwy. 50 American River Canyon.

Guests can choose from cozy cabins and vacation homes featuring 1-4 bedrooms, fully equipped kitchens, fireplaces or woodstoves, decks, and views; some with TVs, telephones, BBQs, jacuzzis, washers and dryers.

Accommodations are conveniently located close to the new Sierra at Tahoe, Heavenly Valley, Kirkwood, and Homewood ski resorts.

Desolation Wilderness, South Lake Tahoe, casinos, shopping, dining, dancing, snowmobiling, snow shoeing, cross-country skiing, horseback riding, hiking, golfing, fishing, hunting, swimming, and water skiing are all only moments away!

High Sierra Getaways offers something for everyone.

As John Muir once stated "Going to the mountains is going home."

Holiday House

P.O. Box 229
7276 N. Lake Blvd.
Tahoe Vista, CA 96148
(530) 546-2369
(800) 2 WINDSURF
Owner: Alvina Patterson

Accommodations: Lakefront suites.

Amenities: Magnificent view, buoys, private beach, hot tub, and swimfloat.

Rates: $95.00 - $185.00 per night; weekly $705.00 - $1050.00

Minimum Stay: One night (weekly). Two nights (weekend). Three nights (holidays).

Restrictions: $10.00 each additional person.

Holiday House is a cozy retreat with six lakefront suites and one spacious two bedroom two bath suite with kitchen in the back. Each lakefront suite has a separate bedroom (queen or king bed), a living room with queen hide-a-bed and a fully equipped kitchen, cable TV, telephone, panoramic view, decks, and barbecue.

From your lakefront lodging, enjoy world-famous ski areas from Squaw Valley to Mount Rose. We are seven minutes away from Nevada gambling and nightlife. A public bus and free ski shuttle is available.

Winter activities include downhill and cross-country skiing, and snowmobiling. Summer sports include swimming, golf, tennis, bicycling, hiking, fishing, waterskiing, boating, sailing, windsurfing, rafting, and horseback riding.

During the summer, you may learn to windsurf or rent boards. The small windsurfing school is run by certified instructor, Alvina Patterson. Generally, there are calm or no winds in the morning and thermal southwest winds in the afternoon.

Tahoe Vista is on Lake Tahoe's north shore, which is famous for it's beautiful mountain and lake views. It is more quiet and closer to nature than the bustling south shore with it's big casinos. There are outstanding restaurants within walking distance and many sandy public beaches.

Holiday House - your year round destination for beauty, relaxation, and fun!

Rustic Cottage Resort

P.O. Box 18
7449 N Lake Blvd.
Tahoe Vista, CA 96148
(530) 546-3523
(888) 7RUSTIC
www.rusticcottages.com
Owner: Janet & Marshall Tuttle

Accommodations: 18 cozy housekeeping cottages on 2 acres plus a 3 bedroom vacation home. Open all year.

Amenities: Private bathrooms, fireplaces with all basic supplies, refrigerators, microwaves, coffeemakers, decks, BBQ's, lawn and picnic areas, croquet, horseshoes, and bicycles. Continental breakfast, homemade baked goodies. Large meeting room. Beach access.

Rates: $59.00 - $235.00 per night.

Minimum Stay: One night in cottages. Two nights in house.

Restrictions: Nice, happy people only. Smoking allowed outdoors only. Pets okay in some cottages for an additional $10.00 per night with prior arrangements.

The Rustic Cottage Resort is located in Tahoe Vista on Lake Tahoe's north shore just a stone's throw from the water's edge. Originally the sawmill and labor camp of the Brockway Lumber Company, the property converted to vacation cottages in 1925. The 18 "Old Tahoe" cottages are all different in size and layout each with it's own character.

Most cottages have kitchens, some have fireplaces, and many have both. All cottages have romantic Benicia iron beds with beautiful linens, Serta mattresses, TV/HBO and VCRs, as well as refrigerators, microwave ovens, coffeemakers, and beautiful patio furniture on the decks.

Lake Tahoe is famous for fun. The community of Tahoe Vista is centrally located and has many great restaurants, sandy public beaches with boat launching facilities, a regional park, and a marina with boat, kayak, and bicycle rentals. The Rustic Cottage Resort is just minutes away from hiking, golf, tennis, mountain biking, horseback riding, shopping, North Shore casinos, ice skating, sledding, and the world's best skiing.

All of our guests are invited to start the day with a complimentary continental breakfast featuring homemade muffins. Try your hand at croquet or horseshoes, borrow a movie from our video tape library, or stop by the office in the afternoon for homemade chocolate chip cookies and other goodies.

For reservations or more information about visiting Lake Tahoe and the Rustic Cottage Resort, give us a call or check out our website.

Sorensen's

14255 Hwy. 88
Hope Valley, CA 96120
(530) 694-2203
(800) 423-9949
Owner: John Brissenden

Accommodations: 1 double room with bath; 2 double rooms share a bath, 28 housekeeping cabins, each accommodating 2-8 persons.

Amenities: Restaurant, wood-burning stoves, convenience store, sauna, trout pond, picnic tables, BBQs, and children's play area.

Minimum Stay: Two nights (weekends). Three-four nights (holidays).

Restrictions: No smoking. Pets permitted in two cabins.

If you ever wanted to go camping in the High Sierra and didn't like the idea of sleeping on the ground, Sorensen's is a good alternative. A historic mountain resort lying alongside the Carson River, at the 7,000 foot level just east of Carson Pass, open year-round, Sorensen's offers access to 600 square miles of public land, mountain scenery, hiking trails, fishing streams, star-laden nighttime skies, and fields of summer wildflowers. The inn provides comfortable accommodations, ranging from fairly primitive to classy, in bed & breakfast units, and housekeeping cabins. Some of the latter date from the turn of the century, when Martin Sorensen, an immigrant Danish shepherd, and his wife, Irene, began camping here. For more than 50 years, the place was a summer hangout for wilderness folk, fishing people, and family friends.

Sorensen's Resort is an eclectic collection of accommodations connected by a network of trails, log cabins in the woods, rustic cedar-sided cabins, even a replica of a 13th-century Norwegian house. Most of the cabins have kitchens; many have separate sitting areas and sleeping lofts. Cabins are offered on a housekeeping basis, but there are small, simply furnished bed and breakfast rooms as well. Guests select breakfast from the menu at the Country Cafe, housed in a log cabin and open for all three meals.

Not only does Sorensen's offer accommodations for outdoor lovers, they also try to enhance your understanding of it all with classes in fishing and fly-tying. Guests can hike along the historic Emigrant Trail (which passes through the property), study the stars, and cross-country ski throughout the winter.

Tamarack Lodge

P.O. Box 859
Tahoe City, CA,   96145
(530) 583-3350
(530) 583-3531 FAX
e-mail: eugene@tamarackattahoe.com
www.tamarackattahoe.com
Owners: Eugene & Marilyn French

Accommodations: Cabin with 2 bedrooms, 2 bathrooms
kitchen and living room; studio cabins with kitchenettes,
1 and 2 bedrooms.

Amenities: Forest setting, cable TV, coffeemakers, telephones,
nearby beaches, and ski areas.

Rates: $39.00 to $120.00 per night.

Minimum Stay: One night.

Restrictions: No pets. Smoking allowed in some rooms.

Nestled among evergreen trees on a 4-acre knoll, Tamarack
Lodge provides it's guests with a quiet haven of rest after
enjoying an active day at Lake Tahoe's North Shore. The short
distance from Tahoe City isolates this motel from the hustle and

bustle of downtown, yet it is close enough to allow our guests to get there on foot, bicycle, auto, or bus. Tamarack Lodge is surrounded by forest which you can explore on foot or mountain bike.

From the "poker" rooms and cabins with kitchenettes, lined in richly finished knotty pine, with queen-sized beds, to the two bedroom, two bath cabin with kitchen and living room, all accommodations feature firm beds, and cable TV with commercial free movies. Other rooms have a king bed or two queen beds and some have kitchens.

Built in the 1920's, the original establishment had a row of rooms and a few cabins clustered around the main building which housed a speak-easy and a dining room with a large free-standing, rock fireplace. Heavy snows in the winter of 1932 collapsed the main building never to be rebuilt, leaving only the fireplace as a link to our romantic past. When it seems right, any time of year, there will be a fire in the old fireplace, where we gather to greet old friends and meet new ones.

Lady Luck was frequently present at the Tamarack. History has it that Hollywood celebrities (Clark Gable, Gary Cooper and Wallace Beary) came to hunt, fish, and play poker. This led to the original row of rooms being called "Poker Rooms".

Tamarack Lodge is centrally located in the North Tahoe area providing easy access to the full range of summer and winter activities, excellent restaurants, sight-seeing, and gaming. At Tamarack, our goal is always *"Hospitality...the way it used to be!"*

Zephyr Cove Resort

P.O. Box 830
Zephyr Cove, NV   89448
(775) 588-6644
(775) 588-5021 FAX
e-mail: 2cr@tahoedixie2.com
www.tahoedixie2.com
Owners: Travel Systems, LTD

Accommodations: 24 cabins, 7 lodge rooms, RV & tent sites.

Amenities: A mile of sandy Lake Tahoe beach, general store, restaurant, beach bar, M.S. Dixie II cruises, woodwind sailing cruises, boat rentals (pedal to ski boats), jet skis, parasailing, sportfishing charters, snowmobile center, BBQs, picnic areas, and beach volleyball courts.

Rates: $80.00 - $295.00 per night (cabins); $50.00 - $100.00 per night (lodge rooms).

Minimum Stay: One night. Some two night minimums apply.

Restrictions: None.

Just four miles from the bright lights and high-rise glamour of Stateline's casinos, Zephyr Cove Resort offers visitors the feeling of "old Tahoe". Owned by the U.S. Forest Service and operated by Travel Systems, Ltd., Zephyr Cove's accommodations feature 24 cabins ranging from studios to four bedrooms nestled along the Lake's shore. Many of the cabins offer lake views and fireplaces, and all are just steps from one of Tahoe's favorite beaches. Rustic lodge rooms and a large RV park and campground are also available.

The property contains a general store and family-style restaurant in the main lodge, guided horseback riding on lakeview trails, and in the winter is home to the west coast's largest snowmobile tour center. Don't worry! The tours actually ride several miles away so you won't hear snowmobiles from your cabin.

In summer, with a mile of sandy beach, Zephyr Cove is one of Tahoe's most popular beaches. It's marina is home port of the M.S. Dixie II, Tahoe's newest and largest paddlewheeler; and the Woodwind II, a 49 passenger catamaran. Rental boats, from pedal boats to ski boats are also available, as are jet ski rentals, parasail rides, and sportfishing charters. A gift shop and the Sunset Beach Bar, volleyball courts and large picnic areas round out the beach's amenities. With activities galore, it's the ideal summer spot for families and groups with varied interests.

In spring and fall, Zephyr Cove takes on a completely different character as the summer excitement is replaced by off season tranquility. Guests can enjoy a quiet sunset and gain a real understanding of why Mark Twain called Lake Tahoe "the fairest picture the earth affords..."

SOUTHERN CALIFORNIA

The Alisal Guest Ranch and Resort

1054 Alisal Road
Solvang, CA 93463
(805) 688-6411
(800) 425-4725
(805) 688-2510 FAX
Owners: The Jackson Family

Accommodations: 73 cottages with woodburning stoves and private baths.

Amenities: Pool, hot tub, two 18-hole championship golf courses, tennis, private lake, and horseback riding.

Rates: $295.00 - $380.00 for two persons per night (includes breakfast and dinner); $40.00 - $65.00 for each add'l person.

Minimum Stay: Two nights.

Restrictions: No pets.

Set in 10,000 unspoiled acres of the beautiful Santa Ynez Valley, the Alisal Guest Ranch and Resort takes guests back in style to the days when the Old West was at its most romantic. Surrounded by gently rolling hills that are golden in the summer and emerald green with splashes of wildflowers in the spring, the Alisal is generously populated with eagles, deer, and occasional coyotes and mountain lions. Huge century-old oaks dot the hillsides, but it is the sycamores that gave the place its name. In Spanish, Alisal means "grove of sycamores," and the Native Americans named the area after the large number of these sprawling trees were found in the valley.

Only 40 miles north of Santa Barbara, the Alisal blends the rustic charm of a working cattle ranch with first class accommodations in 73 guest cottages with woodburning fireplaces, enhanced by fine dining and extensive recreational facilities.

Some guests choose this large spread for the horseback riding through rolling and scenic ranchlands; others for the two 18-hole championship golf course in a setting of oaks, sycamores, and eucalyptus. Still other vacationers come for the combination of tennis (seven courts), beautiful swimming pool and spa, boating, windsurfing, and other water sports on the 100-acre spring-fed lake, and the hospitable family feeling at this historic ranch. An extensive year round children's program for all ages is provided with special evening programs in summer and holidays as well as a full range of games including shuffleboard, horseshoes, badminton, croquet, billiards, fishing, water sports, and biking.

The Santa Ynez Valley abounds with wineries, thorough-bred horse ranches, art galleries, outdoor theater from May - October, and the nearby village of Solvang, the Danish capital of America, with major shopping opportunities.

Arrowhead Pine Rose Cabins

"The Besty Ross"

25994 Hwy. 189
P.O. Box 31
Twin Peaks, CA 92391
(909) 337-2341
(909) 337-0258 (FAX)
Owners: David & Tricia DuFour

Accommodations: 15 cabins (4 studios, 3 one-bedrooms, 4 two-bedrooms, 2 three-bedrooms, and 1 five-bedroom).

Amenities: Kitchens, some woodburning fireplaces, swimming pool, and play areas with recreational equipment.

Rates: $49.00 - $325.00 per night.

Minimum Stay: Two nights on weekends. Three nights on holidays.

Restrictions: Pets allowed in certain cabins.

Innkeepers David and Tricia DuFour invite you to make a special memory in one of our fifteen uniquely decorated theme cabins. Nestled among five acres of forest each cabin comes complete with linens, fully equipped kitchens (with full size refrigerators), color TV's, and BBQ's.

All the cabins are decorated in mountain themes. Some of our themes include "Christmas", "Wild Bills" with a covered wagon bed, "Indian Outpost" with a teepee bed and our honeymoon cabin called "Rustic Romance" with a jacuzzi tub and large stone fireplace. All of our cabins are warm and cozy with pine interiors and real woodburning fireplaces. With a variety of styles and sizes of cabins, we're sure to have one for your individual needs.

We are centrally located between Lake Gregory (3 miles to the west), and Lake Arrowhead (3 1/2 miles to the east). We're within walking distance to the historic log restaurant called "The Antlers". We offer fishing, hiking, ice-skating, horseback riding, skiing, archery, a rifle range, and a waterslide. You many want to just relax by our large heated pool (open May - September), or play volleyball, giant checkers, croquet, horseshoes, or shuffleboard. Or maybe you would like to take a walk through our forested property.

Whether you are a family or a couple, active, or in need of relaxation among the pines, Arrowhead Pine Rose Cabins is the place for you. We can accommodate weddings up to 100 and are known as a popular spot for family reunions.

We are only 1 1/2 to 2 hours from most southern California cities. Ask about our ski packages, hiking packages, and wedding packages.

Brookside Farm Bed & Breakfast

1373 Marron Valley Rd.
Dulzura, CA 91917
(760) 758-0831
Owners: Edd & Sally Guishard

Accommodations: 10 rooms complete with full breakfast.

Amenities: Gourmet dinners, queen beds, private baths, beautiful gardens, and stream.

Rates: $65.00 - $115.00 per night.

Minimum Stay: Two nights.

Restrictions: Not recommended for children. No smoking. No pets.

Brookside Farm is located on Marron Valley Road, near Engineer Springs, in Dulzura, a backcountry community about 30 miles east of downtown San Diego on State Route 94, and ten highway miles from the Mexican border town of Tecate.

This country-style Bed and Breakfast has ten rooms. Five of the rooms are located in the farmhouse proper, along with a sunny sitting room and library, a dining room with a large stone fireplace, a piano and an old-fashioned windup Victrola, and a warm, homey kitchen where the meals are prepared.

Adjacent to the farmhouse is a huge stone and barrel-roof barn, housing two more guest rooms and two upstairs luxury suites. Additionally, two cottages - one perched at the very edge of the creek, and one atop a sunny knoll are available as well.

Each of the Farm's ten bedrooms expresses a personality of its own, and is furnished with appropriate period pieces, handmade quilts, and hand-woven rugs, in keeping with the room's motif.

A spa is available for guest use as well as four acres of colorful and inviting grounds to play volleyball, badminton, croquet, horseshoes, or to just relax.

The Inn also provides a large assortment of books, puzzles, and games for indoor recreation.

Edd's finely-honed culinary skills are showcased each morning in his hearty country-style breakfasts, and on weekends in the four-course dinners optionally available to the Farm's guests. Sally is responsible for all the homemade goodies -- breads, rolls, cakes, and pies.

For those guests interested in taking a short trip, the border town of Tecate is close by with its quaint plaza with Mexican bargains in pottery and handmade artifacts or to sample native cuisine.

Buckskin Landing

34672 Navajo Road
Julian, CA 92036
(760) 366-2413
Owners: John & Judy Bucko

Accommodations: 2 story cabin (sleeps 2 upstairs and 4 downstairs).

Amenities: Small but complete kitchen, TV, VCR, stereo, brick fireplace with stove, deck overlooking lake, boating, fishing, and hiking.

Rates: $80.00 (upstairs only) - $100.00 per night (entire cabin).

Minimum Stay: Two nights. Discounts for extended stay.

Restrictions: No pets. Smoking outside only.

A Northern California climate exists only one hour from San Diego. Buckskin Landing, located at 5000 feet in the Cleveland National Forest, overlooks Lake Cuyamaca with oak and pine covered mountain peaks making a beautiful backdrop. Buckskin Landing is a 2-story cabin of 1000 sq. ft. with a lawn shaded by century old oaks and young pines. Nicely furnished with sleeping for 6, the upstairs has a brick fireplace, color TV/VCR/stereo, a bathroom, kitchen, dining room, queen Murphy bed, sofa bed and a deck with barbecue and view. A pitched cedar ceiling gives outdoor ambiance while soft lighting makes the nights cozy. The downstairs consist of one large room with two fullsize beds, TV/VCR/stereo and a view. Firewood is provided and electric heat picks up where the sun and a cozy fire leave off. Fresh linens and comforters are supplied on the beds but we don't supply bath towels, toiletries, or perfect weather.

Lake Cuyamaca has boat launching and boats to rent. Bass, trout, catfish, and sunrises can be caught on the lake or at the Lake Store Restaurant. Nearby trails offer scenic viewing for hikers, mountain bike, and horseback riders. A weekend would not be complete without a visit to Julian, a 19th century gold mining town, only eight miles away. Renowned for it's orchards, apple pie, operating goldmine, old west architecture, quaint shops and restaurants, it has become a year round destination area.

For those with more time, a half hour to one hour of driving will take you to places like Anza-Borrego State Park, Mt. Palomar Observatory, Warner Springs Glider Center, Tecate and San Diego with it's beautiful harbor, world famous San Diego Zoo, U.S. Navy & Marine Corp bases, and miles of beaches.

Chillon Chalet

996 Chillon
Crestline, CA 92325
(818) 782-0335
(818) 376-0070
Owners: Paul Ramond & Ken Junod

Accommodations: 3 bedroom, 2 1/2 bath three-level home. Sleeps up to 12 comfortably.

Amenities: Kitchen with dishwasher and microwave, laundry facilities, cable TV/VCR, and stereo with CD player.

Rates: $165.00 per night plus minimum cleaning fee of $45.00.

Minimum Stay: Two nights.

Restrictions: No pets. Smoking in restricted area only.

Located high in the fresh air of the San Bernardino Mountains between Lake Arrowhead and Crestline, Chillon Chalet is a spacious mountain retreat with a fabulous view, beautiful stone fireplace, cathedral ceilings and large sun decks.

The house includes three bedrooms, a loft, 2 1/2 baths and a dining area that accommodates twelve. It features all of the comforts of home - laundry facilities, cable TV, stereo, central dining area that accommodates twelve, central heat, linens and towels, a modern kitchen with dishwasher, microwave and a pantry stocked with staples.

A short two hour drive from Los Angeles or San Diego, the house is secluded among firs and cedars. Yet it is still close to conveniences such as markets, shops, movie theaters, and fine restaurants.

It is ideal for family fun or as a great romantic getaway for two. Year round recreational activities are available nearby: snow skiing, ice skating, boating, fishing, swimming, bowling, horseback riding, and hiking. You can stroll down the main street in the quaint town of Crestline which is lined with charming boutiques and antique shops, or just snuggle up in front of the huge stone fireplace after a day of browsing or recreational fun.

The Cottage

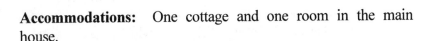

3829 Albatross St.
San Diego, CA 92103
(619) 299-1564
(619) 299-6213 FAX
Owners: Robert & Carol Emerick

Accommodations: One cottage and one room in the main house.

Amenities: King size bed, private bath, private entrance, and woodburning stove.

Rates: $65.00 - $125.00 per night for 1-2 people.

Minimum Stay: Two nights.

Restrictions: Smoking outside only. No pets.

The Cottage is a quiet retreat in the heart of San Diego. Located on a cul-de-sac in the Hillcrest section of town, the homestead style house is one of many homes in the area built around the turn of the century. Canyons dominate the neighborhood so one does not feel they are in the middle of the 6th largest city in the U.S. Hillcrest is a pleasant walking neighborhood. Four blocks from The Cottage there is an assortment of many good restaurants, several theaters, used bookstores, and shops. The

San Diego Zoo, Balboa Park, Sea World, Old Town and Horton Plaza, the Amtrak Station, and the Convention Center are all within a three mile radius of The Cottage. Public transportation is just a few blocks away.

The Cottage is a complete small house located behind a 1913 homestead style home. Surrounded by furnishings from the late 1800's and early 1900's, you will be comfortably accommodated in a king size bed. A full private bath and a fully equipped kitchen complete the cozy ambiance of The Cottage.

The Garden Room is located in the main house, adjacent to patio. The private entrance, private full bath, and king size bed are for your exclusive use.

Each morning you will be served freshly baked bread, juice or locally grown fruit, and freshly roasted Pannikin coffee or exotic and herbal teas.

Enjoy the herb garden surrounding The Cottage. Sages, mints, lavenders, and 30 more herbs are in various stages of bloom year round. There are several places to sit in the garden when you are not busy sightseeing.

The Cottage has been inspected, rated, and approved by the American Bed and Breakfast Association and AAA.

The Forrester Homes

38850 Newberry St.
Cherry Valley, CA 92223
(800) 587-5576
(909) 845-1004
(909) 845-1004 FAX
Owners: Richard & Bonnie Forrester

Accommodations: Completely furnished cabin, cottage and chalet to accommodate 2 to 25 persons.

Amenities: Kitchens, BBQs, TVs, VCRs, maid service, and fireplaces.

Rates: $335.00 - $440.00 for two nights on weekends (includes linens, firewood, and beach access).

Minimum Stay: Two nights.

Restrictions: Small trained dogs permitted. No smoking. No loud parties.

Lake Arrowhead is a year round resort community that is the most popular mountain destination for Southern Californians. It is located about 20 miles north of San Bernardino at 5500 feet in the San Bernardino Mountains. This first class alpine community of 27,000 residents offers lake recreation in the summer and ski facilities and services in the winter. There is lots to do and see in the village and surrounding mountain community.

The Forrester Homes are among the most sought after recreational lodgings in the area. These homes are frequented by famous personalities and are known for their professional decorations, cleanliness, and casual elegance. Our lodgings are recommended by the Chamber of Commerce of Lake Arrowhead, Inland Empire Tourism Council, and the San Bernardino Convention and Visitor's Bureau.

The "Cedar House" sleeps six and is a perfect weekend retreat for a couple or two with or without children. The "Highland House" is a charming mountain retreat, which also sleeps six, and is designer furnished and in pristine condition. The "Lodge" is the epitome of mountain estates available for vacation rental and will comfortably accommodate up to sixteen people.

Owner Richard Forrester is a member of Vacation Rental Managers Association and is listed in Who's Who in Finance & Industry. The Forrester Homes of Lake Arrowhead provide the ideal environment in which to regroup, recharge, revitalize, and renew yourself. Kick back and relax or plan the ultimate in a self-directed fitness vacation through aerobics, fitness walks, running, biking, swimming, and hiking. The air is fresh and fragrant. The sky is the limit in Lake Arrowhead.

Green Valley Lake
Cozy Cabin Rentals

33287 Wild Cherry Drive
P.O. Box 8345
Green Valley Lake, CA 92341
(909) 867-5335
(909) 867-5188
Owners: Bill & Sue Pope

Accommodations: Fifty mountain homes.

Amenities: Completely furnished with fully equipped kitchens, fireplaces or woodburning stoves and basic gas or electric heat.

Rates: $160.00 - $450.00 per night.

Minimum Stay: Two nights.

Restrictions: No pets are allowed in some cabins. No smoking allowed in most cabins.

Small, serene and secluded, Green Valley Lake is situated in the heart of the San Bernardino National Forest. Two hours from Los Angeles and less than three hours from San Diego, Green Valley Lake is four miles off Hwy. 18, equidistant from Lake Arrowhead and Big Bear Lake. At 7200 feet, Green Valley Lake is the highest community in the San Bernardino mountains.

A small, seven acre lake is the focal point of the community. It provides areas for fishing, swimming, and non-motorized boating in the summer. Bike paths and hiking trails intertwine the area in and around the community. In the winter cross-country skiing and snowboarding facilities are available in Green Valley Lake, and for downhill skiing, Snow Valley is a short seven miles away.

As a year round resort, Green Valley Lake's most important attribute is the peace and tranquility it provides even though large urban and suburban areas are close by.

Green Valley Lake/Cozy Cabin Rentals have fifty privately owned cabins under contract for weekend and weekly rentals. The cabins vary in size from one bedroom to five bedrooms, each with a maximum number of persons it will accommodate. The cabins are individually decorated by the owners and as such run the gamut from very rustic to impeccable. Most have cable TV. Many have microwaves and washers and dryers. Renters must provide their own linen, paper products, firewood, and plastic bags for trash. A $100 refundable cleaning/security deposit is required as well as the rental fee.

Green Valley Lake has a small market, three restaurants, a lumberyard/hardware store, and a video rental shop. The closest ATM machine and service station is seven miles away in Running Springs.

Call or write for free literature on Green Valley Lake and a list of cabins with pricing. Call us for a truly "great escape".

Knotty Pine Cabins

54340 Pine Crest
P.O. Box 477
Idyllwild, CA 92549
(909) 659-2933
Owners: Robert & Yvonne Palmer
Managers: Ed & Sandy Reed

Accommodations: 8 cabins and duplex cabins.

Amenities: Kitchens, fireplaces, VCRs, BBQ's, horseshoes, volleyball, badminton, and nearby hiking and fishing.

Rates: $56.00 - $130.00 per night.

Minimum Stay: Two nights on weekends.

Restrictions: Pets in some units for a $10.00 fee.

If you're in southern California, you don't have to fly in an airplane or drive your car for several hours to find a mountain getaway where you can experience clean air, rugged scenery and small town life. About 100 miles from the Los Angeles or San Diego areas (yet seemingly in another country), Knotty Pine Cabins is in the San Jacinto Mountains, a short walk from the village of Idyllwild. At an altitude of 5300 feet, we experience snow in the winter months and cooler summer temperatures, making for a versatile year round retreat.

There are eight cabins and duplex cabins, each one special in its own way, ranging from a one room cabin with fireplace up to our three bedroom cabin called Security Lodge. All are cozy and comfortable, ready to make you feel at home. Completely furnished and well-equipped, you will find your cabin has everything necessary for a pleasant stay, whether it's just for one day or for a week or two.

The grounds at Knotty Pine Cabins are naturally beautiful with lots of tall pine trees, oak trees, manzanita bushes, and other native Idyllwild greenery. You might enjoy feeding the many birds and squirrels, reading a book on the pine-shaded gazebo, playing volleyball, badminton, or horseshoes, or playing in the snow during the winter. As evening comes around, how about a barbecue and then a moonlit walk under the endless field of stars.

There are many hiking trails nearby, going up into the rugged San Jacinto Mountain wilderness, offering easy walks to moderate and more strenuous hikes. Try your luck fishing in two local lakes, Lake Hemet and Lake Fulmor, or stream fishing in Strawberry Creek. Or how about a short walk into the village to check out the various shops and restaurants or see our famous totem pole monument. If you choose to just step out your door and walk around the spacious grounds around the cabins, be sure to keep your eyes open to see our "raccoon family in a den", "giant ivy" and the "woodpecker tree".

McGilvray House

2506 C Street
Julian, CA 92036
(800) 7-JULIAN
e-mail: Sstairway@aol.com
www.geocities.com/julianmcgilvrayhouse/
Owners: Camey, Ian & Emily McGilvray

Accommodations: Fully-equipped vacation cottage.

Amenities: Fireplace, cable TV.

Rates: $85.00 per night on weekends; $75.00 per night on weekdays.

Minimum Stay: Two nights.

Restrictions: Smoking outside only. Pets must be approved.

Our charming red cottage is located in the townsite of Julian on the corner of C Street and 2nd Street. It is quiet and private, but is located within walking distance to everything in Julian.

McGilvray House can comfortably accommodate a couple, or a family, or group of up to five people. The bedroom has a queen size bed and the living room has a queen size futon and a single futon for extra guests. We have a fully-equipped kitchen, bathroom with shower, woodburning fireplace and cable TV. Linens and towels are provided.

Julian is a quaint, 100 year-old gold-mining town. You can get a flavor of Julian's past by touring the Eagle Gold Mine and visiting the Pioneer Museum. Julian has a population of 500 people. The elevation is about 4200 feet and most winters we get some snow.

At McGilvray House, you can sit on the big front porch and just relax. The property is fenced all around and has many plants, flowers, and trees. In season, help yourself to pears, apples, and apricots. You can choose to eat outside on the deck, which is equipped with a picnic table and barbecue.

Take a short stroll down into town. Browse through the bookstore, antique stores, and gift shops. Sample our famous apple pie or have an old-fashioned ice cream sundae. Horse-drawn carriages are available for area tours. The Town Hall Calendar directs you to special events, such as the bicycle races, fiddle contests, and arts and crafts shows. In the fall, special Apple Days activities are scheduled every weekend. Outdoor enthusiasts can take advantage of the many bike trails, and hiking and fishing at nearby Lake Cuyamaca.

There are many things to do and see in Julian and it is most enjoyable to relax and unwind at The McGilvray House.

Panamint Springs Resort

Death Valley National Park
Hwy. 190
P.O. Box 395
Ridgecrest, CA 93556
(775) 482-7680
e-mail: Panamint@ix.netcom.com
www.deathvalley.com
Owner: Jerry Graham

Accommodations: 14 units (1,2, or 3 beds per room) and a 2 bedroom cottage; private baths; 12 full hook up campsites and 22 tent sites; hot showers and toilets for the use of camping guests.

Amenities: Full service restaurant and bar with top quality home cooked meals. Gasoline and oil sales. 2100' gravel runway for fly-in customers. Death Valley National Park and general desert information available.

Rates: $56.50 - $129.50 per night. $5.00 for pets per night.

Minimum Stay: One night. Two nights on certain holiday weekends.

Restrictions: No smoking inside buildings except in designated smoking motel rooms. All pets on leash at all times.

This small desert resort is located about 12 miles east of the western boundary of Death Valley National Park and is the first lodging available inside the park when entering from the west.

The rooms are clean and well kept and are constantly upgraded to provide the best in comfort and enjoyment for our guests. Our grounds are surrounded by the majestic Panamint Mountain range and the Argus range to the rear. Breathtaking sunsets and sunrises are a part of everyday life here at Panamint Springs Resort.

For the guests who like activity there are ghost towns to explore, a desert waterfall with fern grotto to hike to, plus sand dunes at the end of a long desert hike. Wildflowers in the spring after a wet winter season can be nothing short of stupendous.

Panamint Springs Resort is located about halfway between Mt. Whitney (14,496 feet above sea level) which is the highest spot in the lower 48 states and Badwater in Death Valley (282 feet below sea level) which is the lowest spot.

Panamint Springs Resort is at a 2000 foot elevation and even summer evenings are truly enjoyable while sitting on our huge front porch or on our elevated lawn area. Panamint Springs Resort is the ideal place to use as headquarters while exploring the Panamint Valley and Death Valley.

Pierpont Inn By The Sea

550 San Jon Road
Ventura, CA 93001
(805) 643-6144
(805) 641-1501 FAX
Owners: The Gleichmann Family

Accommodations: 72 spacious rooms, suites, and cottages.

Amenities: Restaurant, pool, tennis court, fishing, hiking, and shopping.

Rates: $99.00 - $179.00 per night.

Minimum Stay: One night.

Restrictions: No pets.

Discover a special place on the California coastline, the legendary Pierpont Inn. The classic California Inn is just an hour from the heart of Los Angeles, in quaint and historic Ventura. The new Pierpont Inn by the Sea recently refreshed its style, keeping the beauty and integrity that made it famous. The Gleichmann family hosts guests with a 65 year tradition of signature service admired by all. From fresh cut flowers in the lobby to a booking for tennis at the club, we pamper and indulge our guests. Adventures and delightful surprises mark your visit to the Inn by the Sea.

The Ventura area is famous for sunshine and cool breezes; it's a sportsman's paradise. The Pierpont Racquet Club offers tennis on location. The Inn can arrange your game at one of numerous nearby golf courses. Order a special picnic basket from our kitchen and enjoy a day at the beach. Fishing, hiking, sailing, or shopping on historic Main Street are minutes away.

Social events and garden weddings create lifetime memories at the Pierpont Inn. Spectacular views, award-winning cuisine and service to generations of families make the Inn a sentimental choice for special people. Set in 6 acres of lush gardens, the 84 rooms, suites and cottages afford a choice of unique guest quarters. In banquet areas to accommodate 10 to 125, we will help you plan every detail of your special function. At the Inn, you can celebrate the important and meaningful gatherings of your life.

Our atmosphere is relaxing and quietly elegant. It is easy to get down to business in our dining areas, board rooms and convention facilities. For corporate travelers and groups, the Inn is the top choice. After accomplishing your task and meeting your goals, the ocean is steps away. A world apart, the Inn is your retreat by the sea.

Pine Knot Guest Ranch

908 Pine Knot Avenue
P.O. Box 3446
Big Bear Lake, CA 92315
(909) 866-6500
(800) 866-3446, (909) 866-6794 FAX
www.pineknotguestranch.com
Owners: Larbi & Gloria Loucif

Accommodations: 8 cabins.

Amenities: In-room double jacuzzis, fireplaces, TV/VCR's, BBQ's, fire pit, mountain bikes, playground, and snow play area.

Rates: $79.00 - $159.00 per night.

Minimum Stay: Two nights (weekends). Three nights (holidays).

Restrictions: No smoking. Pets permitted in one cabin.

If you are looking for a secluded, romantic getaway or a family vacation, Pine Knot Guest Ranch is the place for you. We are in a quiet, forested setting, yet only a five minute walk to the village restaurants and shops, and a 10-15 minute walk to the lake. We have newly built individual cabins with woodburning fireplaces, skylights, and in-room double jacuzzi tubs. Some cabins have full kitchens, others have kitchenettes with a mini refrigerator, toaster, microwave, and a coffeemaker. Charcoal grills are available by each cabin.

In the summer, adult size mountain bikes are available to peddle around town and the lake, or to trail bike into the forest. At night you can gather around our firepit for a marshmallow roast and get to know our other guests.

Children will love feeding carrots to our bunnies and treats to our llamas. Llama walks and picnics are scheduled seasonally. We have a small playground and ample space to run around. In winter our open sloped areas are great for sledding and snow play.

Pine Knot Guest Ranch is situated at about 7,000 feet in a wooded area away from highway traffic and next to the national forest. Nearby trails lead you to beautiful scenery of the lake and surrounding areas.

Local attractions include beaches, marinas with boat rentals and water sports, Alpine Slide and pool, biking trails, horseback riding, petting zoo and more.

Winter offers three well-known ski resorts, two of which are minutes away. We offer guided moonlight cross-country skiing and snow shoeing with complimentary hot chocolate.

There are always special local events on weekends such as the antique car show, jazz festival, Octoberfest, craft fairs, and performing arts. Call us to find out what's going on during the time of your visit.

Rankin Ranch

P.O. Box 36-CC
Caliente, CA 93518
(661) 867-2511
Owners: Helen Rankin,
Bill and Glenda Rankin

Accommodations: 14 rooms (mountain cabins nestled in the lilacs and pines).

Amenities: Maid service, all meals, swimming pool, horses, tennis court and recreation room. American Plan – everything is included.

Rates: $100.00 - $160.00 (adult rate per night), $35.00 - $90.00, (children's rate per night).

Minimum Stay: One night.

Restrictions: No pets. No telephones or TV.

The lure of the western frontier brought 22 year old Walker Rankin Sr. from Pennsylvania to California in the early 1860's. After several endeavors, including gold mining, he settled in Walker Basin in 1863. There he founded Quarter Circle U Rankin Ranch where he raised White Faced Hereford cattle. Today this 31,000 acre cattle ranch is still owned and operated by Helen Rankin and family.

Rankin Ranch has welcomed guests since 1965. People from all over the world have visited this ranch and they enjoy the fact that it's a real working cattle ranch.

The ranch is located deep in the Tehachapi Mountains about 125 miles northeast of Los Angeles. Horseback riding is the favorite activity, but there's lots more to do. Trout fishing, tennis, swimming, volleyball, shuffleboard, ping pong, bicycling, and hiking are some of the other daytime activities.

A special supervised children's program gives mom and dad a chance to relax and enjoy their vacation and watch their children have a great time. During the "regular season", the counselor plans western arts and crafts, nature hikes, scavenger hunts, and picnics. "Indian Day" is a favorite...headbands with feathers and face painting, Indian legends and a hike to a Piute Indian campsite where all the children enjoy playing in the creek! Adults and children love "Sarah's Farm" where they can help bottle feed the baby calves. Each evening is filled with fun...hay wagon rides, barbecues with a horseshoe tournament, bingo with prizes, square dances, and more.

Everything is included in the *American Plan Rate* - lodging in mountain cabins which are nestled in lilacs and pines, three full ranch sized meals each day and horseback riding (starting at age six). Rankin Ranch has been featured in Sunset Better Homes and Gardens, Adventure West, Western Styles, and U.S. News and World Report's video, "10 Best All-American Vacations". The ranch has helped celebrate many family reunions, birthdays and special anniversaries. Western hospitality has been alive and well for over a century at Rankin Ranch. You'll be welcome!

Roads End Resort

Star Route 1
P.O. Box 98
Kernville, CA 93238
(760) 376-6562

Accommodations: 4 housekeeping cabins.

Amenities: Kitchens, some fireplaces, linen and cookware supplied. Restaurant, bar, general stores, and camping area.

Rates: $65.00 per night; $5.00 per night for camping area (February - December).

Minimum Stay: Two nights on weekends (walk-ins welcome). Weekday discounts.

Restrictions: Small pets OK with $ 15.00 (non-refundable) cleaning fee. Pets must be on leash and must be attended to at all times.

There are few places where the Spirit of the Old West lingers more noticeably than here at Road's End Resort. Built in 1922, Road's End is rich with the history of earlier days when the road truly ended right here. Road's End began as a pack station taking hunters into the high country for wild game.

Road's End Resort is conveniently located a few hours from the Los Angeles Basin in the Sequoia National Forest. The warm, dry climate makes white water rafting, fishing, and hiking favorite river sports and nearby Lake Isabella offers other activities. Swimming or floating on the river at Road's End's very own beach is the most popular way to spend the day. Winter brings an occasional snow, but does not hamper access to the resort and deep snow is usually just minutes away.

Built in 1934, each rustic cabin has a unique old-fashioned charm. We proudly boast the absence of telephones and televisions. Fireplaces and outdoor fire pits are available.

The Tenderhouse Restaurant features succulent prime rib, perfectly seasoned steaks and seafood. A hearty mountain breakfast is served on weekends. Winter dining by firelight is a favorite among guests.

Summertime visitors may enjoy sipping refreshing cocktails on the outdoor deck just 20 feet from the river. Winter guests can keep warm while sitting by the stone fireplace in the lounge.

We offer a "kitchen sink" selection of camping and fishing supplies at reasonable prices. Fishing tips are free.

Great fishing, giant redwoods, hiking trails, scenic meadows ,and cascading waterfalls are all nearby.

If you just can't "bear" the freeway traffic, smog and stress .... it's "bearly" a drive to the Road's End Resort.

Sleepy Hollow Cabins and Motel

24033 Lake Dr.
P.O. Box 632
Crestline, CA 92325
(909) 338-2718
(800) 909-2718
e-mail: cabins4you@aol.com
www.theplacetorelax.com
Owners: Ralph & Dorie Reeder

Accommodations: 8 cabins, 11 motel rooms, and an executive suite.

Amenities: Cabins with full kitchens and fireplaces. Motel rooms with fireplaces, in-room coffee, and compact refrigerators. Grounds offer seasonal swimming pool, hot tub, and playground All units have telephones. Owners on site.

Rates: $60.00 - $140.00 per night.

Minimum Stay: Two and three nights on select holidays and special events. Weekly rates are available.

Restrictions: No pets.

Sleepy Hollow Cabins is the place to get away from it all.

Although just minutes from the San Bernardino or Victorville areas, it seems a world away. Various majestic pines and giant oak trees welcome visitors to relax. A short walk to Lake Gregory and home to chipmunks, grey squirrels, raccoons and many species of birds, Sleepy Hollow soon becomes a family tradition. With cabins named Lazy Owl, Wild Flower, Cozy Corner, Shy Bunny, and others, and accommodations from one to six guests, (63 total), everyone is sure to find a personal favorite.

Our cabins were built at different times – some in the 1940-1950 era, some in the 70's and 90's. Our motel was built in the early 1980's and is a perfect mix of "modern and mountain". Smoking and non-smoking units are available. Cabins receive daily maid service. Bed linen and towels are provided.

Within walking distance is Lake Gregory, barber/beauty salons, bowling, fine dining, movies, shopping and tennis court. Fishing is a favorite sport at Lake Gregory, although, it also offers aqua cycles, swimming, volleyball and a two track 300 ft. water slide. The 86-acre lake is stocked regularly and makes for excellent bass, catfish, and trout fishing.

Sleepy Hollow is centrally located and is in walking distance of most of the annual events held in Crestline such as golf tournaments, fishing derbies, Jamboree Days (July 4th holiday), 5K & 10K runs, and other events. At an elevation of 4800 feet winter snow is also available. Sleepy Hollow's varied accommodations and location make it ideal for sport teams, groups, family reunions, and retreats.

INDEX

IF YOU WOULD LIKE TO ORDER ADDITIONAL COPIES OF *CABINS & COTTAGES OF CALIFORNIA*, (OR IF YOU ARE INTERESTED IN BEING LISTED IN OUR BOOK), PLEASE FILL OUT THE ORDER FORM BELOW.

OUR BOOKS MAKE GREAT GIFTS -- ESPECIALLY FOR FRIENDS AND RELATIVES WHO ENJOY TRAVELING THROUGHOUT CALIFORNIA.

PLEASE ALLOW 2-3 WEEKS FOR DELIVERY.

SEND $16.95 & $2.00 POSTAGE AND HANDLING (CHECK OR MONEY ORDER) TO:

> RUSTIC GETAWAYS
> P.O. BOX 972
> MEADOW VISTA,CA 95722

NAME_____

ADDRESS_____

_____

_____PLEASE SEND ME _____COPY(S) OF CABINS & COTTAGES OF CALIFORNIA. ENCLOSED IS A CHECK OR MONEY ORDER IN THE AMOUNT OF _____.

_____PLEASE SEND ME INFORMATION ABOUT BEING LISTED IN YOUR BOOK.